The Champagne Companion

Companion

The Authoritative Connoisseur's Guide

The Champagne Companion

The Authoritative Connoisseur's Guide

MICHAEL EDWARDS

RUNNING PRESS

PHILADELPHIA · LONDON

A QUINTET BOOK

Copyright © 1994 Quintet Publishing Limited.

All rights reserved under the Pan American and
International Copyright Conventions. First published in
the United States of America in 1994 by Running Press
Book Publishers.
This book may not be reproduced, in whole or in part
in any form or by any means, electronic or mechanical,
including photocopying, recording or by any
information storage or retrieval system now known or
hereafter invented, without written permission from the
Publisher and copyright holder.

9 8 7 6 5 4 3 2 1
Digit on the right indicates the number of this printing

ISBN 1-56138-440-2

Library of Congress Cataloging-in-Publication Number
94-65108

This book was designed and produced by Quintet
Publishing Limited, The Old Brewery, 6 Blundell Street, London N7 9BH

Creative Director: Richard Dewing
Designers: Ian Hunt/Linda Henley
Senior Editor: Laura Sandelson
Photographer: Paul Forrester

Typeset in Great Britain by
Central Southern Typesetters, Eastbourne
Manufactured in Hong Kong by Regent Publishing Services Limited
Printed in China by Leefung-Asco Printers Limited

This book may be ordered by mail from the publisher.
Please add $2.50 for postage and handling.
But try your bookstore first!

RUNNING PRESS
BOOK PUBLISHERS
125 South Twenty-Second Street
Philadelphia, Pennsylvania 19103–4399

PICTURE CREDITS
Abbreviations: pp = pages; b = bottom; l = left; r = right; t = top.
Bollinger: p73. Champagne Bureau: pp22, 23, 55l, 57l, 213b.
Jan Jonker: p33t. Janet Price: pp5, 10, 11, 12, 13r, 22b, 28, 29,
30, 31, 32t, 33b, 34, 35, 47, 61l, 66, 71, 82, 87, 94b, 96, 102, 132t,
133, 138, 160b, 164r, 170r, 174, 177b, 181l, 185t, 190, 194r, 200,
204, 205l, 206, 216l. Mansell Collection: pp8, 14, 74. Moet &
Chandon: pp16, 17, 18, 149. Remy & Assoc.: p15. Tor
Eigeland: pp26, 27, 32b, 218l. Bottles and labels were supplied
by the champagne houses and photographed by Paul Forrester.

Contents

AUTHOR'S ACKNOWLEDGEMENTS

For Barbara, with love.

It would not have been possible to write this book
without the generous help of many merchants and
growers in Champagne who opened their rarest bottles
for me, often at short notice. But I would like to thank
especially the following friends in the trade and press
who gave particular support at times when I most
needed it: Françoise Peretti and Pierre Levron of The
Champagne Information Bureau; Philippe Le Tixerant
of the CIVC; Merlin Holland of *The Oldie*; Dr Teresa
Challoner (a discerning punter); and above all, Yves
Sauboua of Les Saveurs Restaurant, London; Roger Seal
of the British Academy of Gastronomes; and my long-
suffering editors, Laura Sandelson and Helen Varley.

THE STORY OF
Champagne

Brief History

*N*O ONE KNOWS FOR SURE when vines were first planted in Champagne. But there is no doubt that grapes *for wine-making purposes* were being cultivated in this northeastern province of France, at that time Roman Gaul, 50 years after the birth of Christ. Yet just at the time when these vineyards were starting to flourish, a protectionist Roman emperor, Domitian, decreed that they be uprooted. In A.D. 282 one of his successors, Probus, a gardener's son, lifted the ban, and the pleasure-loving Romans soon became partial to the wines of Champagne. The new drink from Gaul must have tasted like the nectar of the gods compared with the dyspeptic Italian wines of the time which, according to the wine writer Patrick Forbes, were often flavored with substances ranging from sea water and pitch to myrtle berries and poppy seeds.

From the fall of the Roman Empire in the 5th century until the birth of the Renaissance in the 15th, the wines of Champagne became steadily more popular with the rich and powerful. One reason for their success was the geography of the province. The valley of the Marne, the central corridor of the Champagne district, lies at a crossroads of northern Europe and has always given the Champenois easy access to important wine markets. But, in the words of wine writer Nicholas Faith, "the convenience of the route along the Marne has brought the inevitable corollary that the valley has always been the natural path of any invader from the east and thus the equally natural scene for major battles against marauders."

The murderous Attila the Hun got his come-uppance in one of the bloodiest battles of all time, fought on Champagne's soil. In A.D. 455 Attila was routed near Châlons-sur-Marne, though not before 200,000 men of all races had lost their lives. During the next millennium the province of Champagne alternated between periods of happy prosperity and miserable deprivation. The city of Reims was burned, pillaged, or razed to the ground on seven occasions between A.D. 450 and 1000, and the wine town of Epernay was devastated no fewer than 25 times between the 7th and 16th centuries. Yet Champagne had its lucky breaks, too.

The windmill at Verzenay overlooking the vineyards of the Montagne de Reims

Attila the Hun   *Louis XIV*

In A.D. 987, Hugh Capet was crowned French king in the cathedral at Reims, establishing that city rather than Paris as the spiritual capital of medieval France. Thirty-seven of Capet's successors came to Reims for their coronations, the last being Charles X, who was crowned in the cathedral in 1825. Reims' saintly status proved a boon for the vineyards. Successive kings made munificent donations to the Marne's monasteries, which became excellent wine-making institutions until the French Revolution of 1789. Early religious orders saw nothing venal in the enjoyment of a glass of wine: an 8th-century rule of the nuns at the Hôtel-Dieu in Reims actually used wine as an incentive for good behavior – the rule stipulated that "if any of the sisters says anything abusive to another or swears wickedly, she shall not drink wine that day."

Until the middle of the 17th century, the idea of a sparkling *vin de Champagne* did not exist. As early as A.D. 800, drinkers were already making the distinction between the *vins de la rivière* from the vineyards above the Marne and the *vins de la Montagne* from the higher slopes of the Montagne de Reims. Both were still wines. The wines from the best sites – such villages as Verzenay, on the Montagne, and Ay, close to the Marne – were as highly prized in the Middle Ages as they are today. By the beginning of the 15th century, wine had replaced wool as the main trade of Reims. At about this time, the first professional wine-brokers, the *courtiers en vins*, emerged and came to control the market.

The Champagne district was devastated again during the Fronde, the appalling civil war of the 1640s and 1650s. But as the 16-year-old Louis XIV acceded to the French throne in 1654, the vineyards entered a new period of great expansion. The Champenois, with a nice feeling for public relations they have shown ever since, shrewdly made a present of their wines to the young king at his coronation. He liked the wines so much that they enjoyed a special royal patronage throughout his 60-year reign. The Sun King reputedly never drank anything else until his last years. Wine writer Patrick Forbes, drawing on Saint-Siméon's *Mémoires*, reveals that Louis' favorite was the red wine of Bouzy, which he obtained from a merchant in Ay called Rémy Berthauld.

Ironically, it was an exiled French nobleman who spread the good word about Champagne's wines outside France. In 1662 the Marquis de St. Evremond was effectively banished to England, where he became a friend of Charles II and the arbiter of French fashion at court. A man of exquisite taste, he refined the way the English ate and drank, and made Champagne wines fashionable. But he was more than an ambassador for the wines of the Marne: supplies were difficult to obtain, as there was no regular direct trade between the Champagne growers and the London wine merchants. St. Evremond was the perfect go-between. In a letter to his friend the Comte d'Olonne in 1671, he sounds like a high-pressure salesman: "Spare no expense in getting some Champagne wines . . . Those of Burgundy have lost their prestige with men of taste: They barely maintain their old reputation with the merchants. There is no province like Champagne which supplies such excellent wines for all seasons."

DOM PÉRIGNON, THE MYTH AND THE REALITY

Pierre Pérignon, a Benedictine monk and head cellarer of the Abbey of Hautvillers between 1668 and 1715, has been dubbed the inventor of what we now prize as sparkling champagne. That a drink now so glamorous, associated with seduction and the good life, could have been created by an ascetic monk makes a pleasantly ironic tale which has been carefully cultivated by the champagne house Moët & Chandon, owners of the abbey of Hautvillers since 1822. It is a romantic myth, for the wines of Champagne had a natural tendency to sparkle.

Then as now, the cold climate of the Champagne country dictated that the grapes had to be picked late in the year; there was simply not enough time for the yeasts, present on the grape skins, to convert the sugar in the pressed grape juice into alcohol before winter put them to sleep. In the early spring, the yeasts woke up, the fermentation started again, releasing carbonic gas (carbon dioxide), which, imprisoned in a stoppered cask, had nowhere to escape, hence the sparkle.

It was probably another community of monks, the Benedictines of St. Hilaire at Limoux in the Languedoc, who first produced a French sparkling wine by what is known as the *méthode rurale* in 1531. This delicious bubbly is still made today under the label *Blanquette de Limoux*. The Champenois, of course, would have you believe that deliberately making their wine sparkle was one of the few genuine revolutions in the history of wine-making, but this so-called revolution was really an evolutionary development that took place over nearly 200 years. As Nicholas Faith puts it, "Dom Pérignon was simply one of the most distinguished 'evolutionaries' in developing the wines of Champagne."

None of this diminishes the Dom's place in history as the father of the modern champagne industry. A highly intelligent and resourceful wine-maker, in Patrick Forbes's words, "he penetrated into the tiniest details of his art with the intuition of a really great man [and] he laid down the basic principles which are still in use today." Yet for him the wine was always more important than the bubbles. The fact that it sparkled was probably a nuisance which he tried to control rather than encourage,

The Dom Pérignon chapel at the Abbey of Hautvillers

and the invention of a bottle strong enough to withstand the pressure of the fizz was not his but that of English glass-makers earlier in the 17th century. Pérignon's real achievement, truly dramatic for his time, was to make a clear still white wine from black grapes. And he was certainly the first to understand that in the cold climate of the Champagne region, blending wines from different vineyards produced a much more distinguished drink than using an unblended wine from a single vineyard. After careful studies and maybe reluctantly, Dom Pérignon made his first sparkling champagne around 1690.

THE VICTORY OF THE BUBBLES

Although a Reims poet wrote glowingly of the silvery *mousse* foam in a glass of champagne in 1712, the final victory of the bubbles was not won for at least another 100 years, following the defeat of Napoleon in 1815. Through the 18th century drinkers of the wines of Champagne divided into two camps: the serious connoisseurs preferred the still wines; the fashionable and frivolous were drawn to the *vins mousseux* (sparkling wines) like moths to a flame. The Champenois seem to have hated the new fizz: in 1713, the merchant Bertin du Rocheret called it an abominable drink, adding "effervescence . . . belongs rightly to beer, chocolate, and whipped cream." Sparkling champagne was dismissed by pundits as a "cork-jumper" and the devil's wine, which of course made it popular at the court of the French Regency, where it became the lubricant of louche supper parties.

Ruinart Coat of Arms in the Crayères (cellars) beneath Reims

The origins of the modern champagne trade really date back to 1728, when Louis XV removed the restrictions on the transport of wine in bottles, which had previously stymied the sale of sparkling wines. The next year saw the foundation of Ruinart, the first recorded champagne-making firm. In 1735 the king introduced laws controlling the size and capacity of the champagne bottle, as well as stipulating that the cork be securely tied down with string. And in 1743 Claude Moët established what was to become the biggest champagne house of all, Moët & Chandon.

The sales of wines from Champagne greatly increased during the 50 years before the French Revolution, and in the last year before 1789, sales doubled to 288,000 bottles. Although a good percentage of these were still wines, the future potential of sparkling wine showed in the price of land in the Côte des Blancs which during the 18th century increased by 800 per-cent: the chalky soil of the Côte, then as now, produced wines that sparkled more vigorously.

The champagne-makers did well out of Napoleon's imperial ambitions in the early 1800s. Wherever the French armies were victorious – Austria, Prussia, Poland – a champagne agent was never far behind to console the locals with his wine and to establish a sales network for future business. Even when Napoleon faced final defeat at Waterloo and the terrify-ing Russian cossacks occupied Reims and Epernay, the agile Champenois turned it to their advantage. The story goes that Jean-Rémy Moët encouraged the Russians to take the wine on

An 18th-century invoice in a Ruinart ledger

Roman steps leading to the Ruinart Crayères (cellars)

the sound commercial principle that they would be back. And so it was. Russia soon became the biggest export customer for the Champagne district after Britain.

And yet in this post-Napoleonic time, sparkling champagne-making was still a primitive affair. The deposit formed inside the bottle could only be removed by decanting its contents in a new bottle – a difficult, messy, and expensive business for a sparkling wine. And the adding of sugar to encourage the wine to sparkle very often resulted in too much pressure inside the bottle, causing it to explode. Two technical innovations in the 19th century solved these problems.

Remuage – riddling the wine into order to coax the deposit toward the cork (see page 31) – had previously been a laborious task, as the *remueur* had to take each bottle out of the rack. Antoine Muller, *chef de caves* (cellar-master) for the Widow Clicquot in the 1818, devised *pupitres*, which were inverted V-shaped desks with holes in them. The bottles were placed neck-down in the holes so that they could be turned and tilted every day until the deposit settled safely on the cork.

*A set of 19th-century engravings showing
traditional champagne-making processes*

But an even greater innovation was an apparatus called the *sucreoenomètre* (literally "wine sugar measure,") which was invented by M. François, a modest pharmacist in Châlons-sur-Marne in 1836. This tool successfully measured the amount of residual sugar left in the still wine prior to its second fermentation. Thereafter the champagne-maker could add just the right amount of sugar to the wine to make it sparkle without generating too much pressure inside the bottle. From this time, sparkling champagne, reliably produced in commercial quantities, came of age.

THE CONQUEST OF WORLD MARKETS

Armed with François' discovery, the champagne trade expanded dramatically between the 1840s and the turn of the century. Early on, many firms came into existence and offered their wines at very low prices. But the public quickly became disillusioned with these cut-price champagnes, which could be sold under any name or label. The result was the growing success of known "brands" in which the drinker might have confidence. Several of the best brand-names were established by German immigrants – the Bollingers, the Krugs, the Heidsiecks, and the Mumms – who were accomplished linguists and thus better equipped to conquer world markets. The Louis Roederer family, originally from Alsace, became a principal supplier of champagne to Russia in the 1840s and 30 years later created their ultra-rich *Cristal* (so named because of its clear-glass bottle) to satisfy the sweet tooth of the Czar.

Until the 1850s all champagne was pretty sweet for reasons of commercial expedience: to meet the growing demand for their sparkling product, the champagne houses invariably added a high dose of sugared liqueur to the wine to make it drinkable within a couple of years of the vintage. But by the 1860s a few firms had begun to label their wines "dry" in response to a new trend, fostered by the British, toward a drier and more mature type of champagne. Bollinger shipped a "very dry" champagne to England in 1865. This wine, though not naturally *brut* (bone dry) by modern standards, was far less

A period export poster for Charles Heidsieck

Portrait: "To the health of the chef"

sweet than most others of the time. The first really dry champagne was the 1874 of Madame Pommery, which took Victorian London by storm. The introduction of such a dry version heralded a revolution for champagne, as thereafter on world markets it came to be seen not as a wine for toasts and desserts but as a drink that might be consumed at any time of the day or night. In the "Naughty Nineties" actresses' admirers drank it from slippers, and champagne buffs wrote a lot of rather tedious poems about their favorite vintages.

The Champenois' flair for self-promotion did not desert them when they turned their eyes across the Atlantic. Patrick Forbes relates that the first important exports of champagne to the United States were made in the late 1830s. More than 50 years later, the House of Mumm, prime specialists in the American market, were selling 850,000 bottles a year with the help of a vast advertising campaign, and in the lavish brothels of New Orleans, "wine" meant champagne, preferably Mumm's Cordon Rouge.

Maybe the most colorful champagne salesman in America was George Kessler, Moët & Chandon's agent. At the New York launching of the German Kaiser's yacht in 1903, Kessler had the chutzpah to substitute a bottle of Moët *White Star* for a bottle of German *Sekt*. The Kaiser was furious, but Moët attracted a lot of welcome publicity in the subsequent court case. In 1906 the shameless Kessler presented a railway carriage full of champagne to the survivors of the San Francisco earthquake. South America was another rich market. At the beginning of the First World War, Chile had the highest per capita consumption of champagne in the world, a position now held by Belgium, a nation of wine-lovers.

THE WAR AGAINST IMITATIONS

As exports grew toward the end of the 19th century, so did imitations of the real thing. Elsewhere in France, as well as in Switzerland and Germany, the name "champagne" was cheerfully appropriated by other sparkling wine producers. In 1882, a document issued by the French Ministry of Agriculture claimed (wrongly) that shipments of champagne to the United States had declined because of the competition from California and on account of poor quality. The incensed Champenois took collective action and on the initiative of the Heidsieck family formed the Syndicat du Commerce des Vins de Champagne, a crucially effective trade association composed of the major houses and the precursor of the *grandes marques*. Its aim was to protect the good name and reputation of champagne.

Although the Syndicat du Commerce was unsuccessful in the United States, where domestic sparkling wine may still be called champagne, it won a court action in 1889 against the *mousseux* producers of Saumur, who argued

The Pink Lady,

*Flying Lady poster from Moët & Chandon's
Far East agent*

that the word "champagne" had entered the public domain and thus referred to the method by which the wine was made sparkling rather than to its geographical origin. The Champenois' victory was a foretaste of contemporary actions against makers of luxury goods wanting to cash in on the name: the house of Yves St. Laurent in 1993 was barred from using the title "Champagne" for one of its perfumes.

THE CHAMPAGNE RIOTS

In 1905 the authorities' attempts to establish the borders of the winefield were met with hostility by the growers, who since 1890 had seen their income from grapes drastically reduced by the devastating effects of phylloxera, the aphid which feeds on the sap of the vine causing it to die. The growers were especially resentful of those unscrupulous merchants who were buying grapes for their *cuvées*, or vintages, from well outside the traditional area of Champagne. The *vignerons*, or growers, from the classic heartland of the Marne claimed that their soil alone was suitable for growing champagne grapes, while the Aube growers in the south asserted that their vineyards were part of the ancient province of Champagne, with Troyes its historic capital. The French government vacillated, tempers flared, and it all ended in tears on April 12, 1911, when the Marne growers ran amok in Ay, looting the cellars of the merchants and emptying barrels of wine into the streets.

But common sense soon prevailed and a compromise was reached. The classic heartland of the Marne would be known as "Champagne" whereas the Aube would be called "Champagne Deuxième Zone." The Aube's second-division status was eventually repealed in 1927, when it became part of an enlarged Champagne winefield.

WAR, PROHIBITION, AND RENEWAL

During the First World War, Reims was bombarded more than 1,000 times by German artillery and had to be completely rebuilt after 1918. The widespread anti-drink mood that followed the Armistice was very bad news for the Champenois. The year before, the important Russian market had already disappeared in the Bolshevik Revolution, and the United States, which before the war had imported 3 million bottles of champagne a year, went "dry" with the advent of Prohibition in 1920. Much of Canada and several Scandinavian countries quickly followed. Then came the Great Depression. By 1932 the champagne houses had enough stock, according to champagne writer Tom Stevenson, to cover sales for the next 33 years and only survived by concentrating on the growing French market.

The growers, unable to sell their grapes, formed the first champagne cooperatives at this time. With the ending of Prohibition in 1934, the industry entered an age of renewal, thanks to Robert-Jean de Voguë, head of Moët & Chandon. De Voguë made the revolutionary proposal that the price of champagne grapes be increased six-fold to ensure a decent living for the growers. De Voguë was nicknamed the "Red Marquis" by some of his reactionary fellow-merchants, but in a real sense he was the saviour of the champagne industry in the years leading to the Second World War. Again, largely on his initiative the Germans were persuaded to establish the *Comité Interprofessional du Vin de Champagne* in 1941. More than 50 years later, the C.I.V.C. is the most effective official wine organization in France, at one moment sitting like Solomon in judgement on the competing claims of merchant and grower, the next acting as a well-oiled propaganda machine for the whole champagne industry. The success of the C.I.V.C., dare one say it, owes a lot to the Germanic virtues of efficiency and attention to detail.

═ *The Champagne World* ═

CHAMPAGNE IN THE 1990S is a business of strong brand images dominated by huge conglomerates. By far the most powerful force in the industry is Moët & Chandon, which accounts for nearly a quarter of all export sales. In 1987, the Moët-Hennessy empire, in a deal of Byzantine complexity, took over the Louis Vuitton luxury goods group with its interests in Veuve Clicquot, Lanson (since sold by Moët), and Pommery. The relentless expansion of this giant super-group (known as L.V.M.H.) has resulted in its control of close to 50 percent of the champagne export market. In fairness, big can be beautiful, as the quality of Moët and Clicquot wines is extremely good for their size.

The other big player is Seagram, the Canadian beverage group, which has near-total control of Mumm, Heidsieck Monopole, and Perrier-Jouët. Until very recently, Perrier-Jouët was a little jewel of a house left in peace to make superb champagnes. Its prestige cuvée, *Belle Epoque*, packaged in a *fin du siècle* bottle enamelled in blue and white flowers, was launched in a Paris nightclub in 1970 to celebrate the 70th birthday of Duke Ellington, and has been a huge success in America ever since. The Seagram marketing touch has looked a lot less sure of late with its decision in 1993 to position Mumm Cordon Rouge, a pretty average champagne, at the top end of the price spectrum.

By contrast, the family-owned Rémy-Martin group from Cognac has not put a foot wrong since the early 1970s when it acquired a majority shareholding in Krug. Henri Krug makes superlative wines by which all others are judged, but the Rémy investment allowed him to buy vineyards, notably the Clos du Mesnil, home to the most complex *Blanc de Blancs* champagnes. In 1985 Rémy-Martin bought Charles Heidsieck and four years later, Piper Heidsieck. Daniel Thibault, *chef de caves* for both houses, fashions champagnes which are a pleasure to drink. Like their maker, they have soul.

Of the independent houses, Laurent-Perrier is the success story of the postwar years. Its president, Bernard de Nonancourt, now in his 70s, is the last in a line of larger-than-life characters who shaped the modern champagne trade before the corporatism of today. A natural leader, who as a young man fought with the French Resistance, de Nonancourt has always surrounded himself with people of rare competence.

*Bernard de Nonancourt of
Laurent-Perrier*

Since taking over the company in 1948, he has increased sales from 80,000 bottles to 7 million bottles, making Laurent-Perrier one of the largest houses in Champagne.

Bernard de Nonancourt has always taken the quality route, showing real courage along the way. His bravest decision was the introduction in 1957 of *Grand Siècle*, a prestige cuvée which was not a vintage wine but a blend of three. It is always a magnificent wine. Recently, Laurent-Perrier has diversified its wine interests, taking a major shareholding in the Burgundy house of Antonin Rodet and the Bordeaux firm of Duclot. In California, the de Nonancourts and the Tancers of Iron Horse are involved in a joint venture to make sparkling wine.

Heirs to an older tradition, three great family-owned champagne houses remain financially sound in the 1990s. Louis Roederer is the most profitable on account of its self-sufficiency in grapes from its 450 acres of choice vineyards. Bollinger makes great champagnes in an uniquely muscular style that has a very loyal following in Britain and the United States. And Pol Roger is maybe the most consistent producer of all, seemingly incapable of releasing a bottle of champagne that is not utterly delicious. Despite all the talk of financial strength and distribution networks, sales of champagne will always be buoyed by the quality of wine in the glass.

= *The Making of Champagne* =

High-wheeled tractors ride above the vines in Champagne at harvest-time

THE RESTRAINED RICHNESS of real Champagne has a lot to do with the cold climate of northern France, where the grapes are grown. The heart of the Champagne region lies 90 miles north-east of Paris. The main area of production is around Reims and Epernay, comprising the Montagne de Reims, the Côte des Blancs and the Vallée de la Marne. The Aube, 70 miles away to the southeast, is rarely talked about by the big houses, but its wines are an important component in their non-vintage blends. Champagne grapes are also grown in smaller vineyards across the Aisne, Seine-et-Marne and Haute-Marne.

It is often said that the vineyards of Champagne constitute one of the smallest wine-growing areas of France. Compared with the vast tracts of vines in the Midi, that is true; yet Champagne is twice the size of Beaujolais or Alsace and regularly produces over 200 million bottles of sparkling wine a year. Sales abroad represent 25 percent of all French A.O.C. (*Appellation d'Origine Contrôlée* – meaning that the wine name is protected by law) wines exported.

Vallée de la Marne

Grapes used to make Champagne

Pinot Noir

Pinot Meunier

Chardonnay

= The Champagne Winefield =

THE CHAMPAGNE WINEFIELD lies 90 miles northeast of Paris and
close to the Belgian border. The main area of production is
centred in the *département* (district) of Marne. The Aube vineyards of Champagne are isolated 70 miles southeast, touching
the border with Burgundy. There are also smaller vineyards
spread out across the *départements* of Aisne, Seine-et-
Marne and Haute Marne. This map shows the loca-
tions of the towns and villages listed in this book,
and groups them roughly within the main vineyard regions of Champagne.

AISNE

VALLÉE DE LA

CHÂTEAU-
THIERRY

MARNE

REIMS

PARIS

VALLÉE DE LA MARNE:

1	Champvoisy
8	Cumières
7	Damery
11	Dizy
3	Dormans
10	Hautvillers
6	Leuvrigny
9	Mardeuil
25	Tours-sur-Marne
5	Villers-sous-Chatillon
2	Vincelles

SÉZANN

COTEAUX
DES
SÉZANNAIS

44
45

vineyard	A4/E50 autoroute
regions	...... key routes
	< rivers
	cities/major towns

COTEAUX DES SÉZANNAIS:

44	Bethon
45	Montgenost

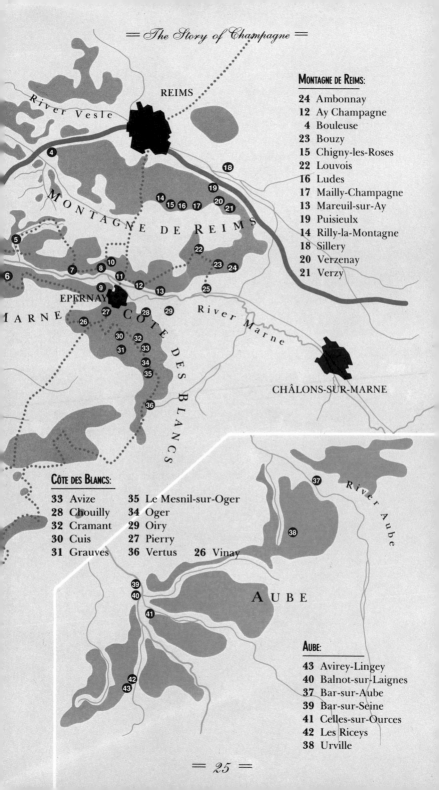

REIMS

River Vesle

MONTAGNE DE REIMS

EPERNAY

CÔTE DES BLANCS

MARNE

River Marne

CHÂLONS-SUR-MARNE

MONTAGNE DE REIMS:

- **24** Ambonnay
- **12** Ay Champagne
- **4** Bouleuse
- **23** Bouzy
- **15** Chigny-les-Roses
- **22** Louvois
- **16** Ludes
- **17** Mailly-Champagne
- **13** Mareuil-sur-Ay
- **19** Puisieulx
- **14** Rilly-la-Montagne
- **18** Sillery
- **20** Verzenay
- **21** Verzy

CÔTE DES BLANCS:

- **33** Avize
- **28** Chouilly
- **32** Cramant
- **30** Cuis
- **31** Grauves
- **35** Le Mesnil-sur-Oger
- **34** Oger
- **29** Oiry
- **27** Pierry
- **36** Vertus
- **26** Vinay

River Aube

AUBE

AUBE:

- **43** Avirey-Lingey
- **40** Balnot-sur-Laignes
- **37** Bar-sur-Aube
- **39** Bar-sur-Seine
- **41** Celles-sur-Ources
- **42** Les Riceys
- **38** Urville

Only three types of grape may be used in the production of champagne. The Pinot Noir, accounting for about 30 percent of the vineyard, is mainly planted on the chalky-sandy hillsides of the Montagne de Reims, and gives wines of richness and finesse. Though prone to rot, it is also increasingly popular in the Aube. The hardier Pinot Meunier is best suited to the warmer soils of the Vallée de la Marne where it is grown for its high yield and spicy flavor. Meunier accounts for nearly half the Champagne vineyard; like the Mafia it is everywhere, but nobody talks about it. This is rather silly, seeing that Meunier is an important source of wines for non-vintage champagnes from the very best houses such as Krug, Roederer, Pol Roger, and Billecart-Salmon. The Chardonnay's natural home is the deep chalk of the Côte des Blancs. Less prone to frost damage than the Pinot Noir, Chardonnay has a higher yield. Refined, elegant, incisive, it is an indispensible component in a champagne blend to balance the greater richness of Pinot Noir. A *Blanc de blancs* champagne is one made purely from Chardonnay grapes.

At harvest time the grapes are carefully picked by hand and sorted to remove damaged berries. This is because most champagne is made from black grapes (Pinot Noir and Meunier), and any damage to the skins could cause discoloration of the must (pressed grape juice). For the same reason the grapes are pressed as quickly as possible in large low presses, about 4 tons at a time. Until the law was amended recently, this

Grape-pickers stripping vines by hand at harvest-time

Traditional low champagne press

Modern champagne presses also de-stalk the grapes

gave about 586 gallons of juice obtained by three separate pressings. The first, the cuvée, produces 451 gallons; the second, the *première taille*, 90 gallons; and the third, the *deuxième taille*, 45 gallons.

The problem is that with each pressing, the must becomes progressively darker and more tannic, and so less desirable. In practice, the best houses only used the *cuvée* (and still do), selling the second and third pressings to cut-price champagne firms. In 1992, the authorities effectively abolished the use of the *deuxième taille* and at the same time reduced the maximum amount of juice permitted from 586 to 560 gallons. The maximum yields of wine per acre are likely to be halved by 1995 in an attempt to reduce stock levels in the future, though many small growers may go out of business in the process.

After pressing, impurities in the must are eliminated by

débourbage, a process which allows solid matter to sink to the bottom of the vat over 12 hours. The clear juice then goes through alcoholic fermentation, which in most cases takes place in stainless steel vats. A few top houses such as Krug, Alfred Gratien, and Bollinger (for its vintage wines) still ferment in wood, and adventurous growers like Anselme Selosse in Avize use 100 percent new oak *barriques* for certain cuvées. At this stage the wine is much like any other still white wine, but the champagne method and the art of blending transform it.

The champagne method is the name for the process of making a wine sparkle by allowing it to ferment for a second time in the bottle. It is now used for quality sparkling wine production throughout the world. But the blender's skill sets champagne apart from lesser wines. Blending requires taste, memory, and experience. The characteristics of the champagne *crus* must be memorized and their flavors married to produce a wine that mirrors the established style of the blender's house. Each year the blender may use a greater or lesser number of wines from the current vintage with a smaller amount of the reserve wines available from previous years.

Once the blend is completed, *liqueur de tirage* (a solution of sugar, old wine, and yeast) is added in carefully measured amounts. The wine is now ready for its second fermentation. The slow process known as the *prise de mousse* will produce a

Stainless steel fermenting vats at Pommery

Small barrique cellar at Krug

Alain Terrier – Laurent-Perrier's chef de caves

Still wines for blending at Louis Roederer

Prince Alain de Polignac of Pommery

Daniel Thibault, chef de caves at Charles Heidsieck

wine with a steady stream of small bubbles in the glass. The pressure created inside the bottle is five or six times that of the atmosphere. As the second fermentation takes place, with the bottles binned on their sides (*sur lattes*), deposits are formed, mostly of dead yeasts, which add complexity to the wine's bouquet and flavor. The length of time that a champagne is allowed to age at this stage is an important factor in its quality. Non-vintage champagne must be aged for at least a year in the bottle before sale, and vintage champagne at least three years. Most good houses age their non-vintage for three years and their vintage for five.

Remuage is a process used to remove the yeast deposits.

Hand remuage

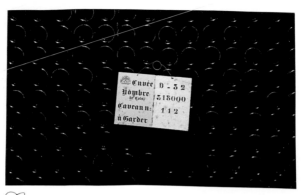

Champagne binned "sur lattes" (the bottles on their sides)

The word means riddling. Traditionally, the bottles are placed in holed racks called *pupitres*, and are turned and tilted every day, eventually arriving at an almost vertical position neck downward. This allows the deposit to settle on the cap or cork. Much of this labor-intensive work is now carried out by automatic machines called *gyropalettes*, which do the job more quickly than *remueurs*, as the skilful men who perform the process are called. However, certain quality-conscious houses, including important ones like Charles Heidsieck, Laurent-Perrier, and Bollinger still prefer the traditional method of riddling by human hand.

At this point, the bottles are taken from the *pupitres* or

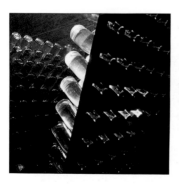

Bottles of Louis Roederer Cristal racked in pupitres, showing the deposit in the neck

Champagne binned "sur pointes" (neck down) for long aging

*Gyropalettes (automatic riddling machines) at
Billecart-Salmon*

*Yeast deposits formed
after second fermentation*

gyropalettes and are stored vertically, upside down, to age gently in preparation for the technique known as *dégorgement*. This simply means removing the cork or cap and releasing the sediment. The bottles in vertical position are passed along a conveyor that freezes the liquid in the neck of the bottle, imprisoning the sediment in a tiny "sorbet" of near-frozen wine. The bottle is then upended by a *dégorgeur* who removes the cap, allowing the pressure of the gas to expel the little block of ice from the wine, which leaves the remainder clear and bright. This technique is known as *dégorgement à la glace*. The old

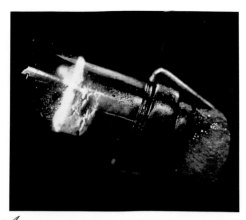

A bottle illuminated to show the deposit in the neck

A cellarman at G. H. Mumm

method of *dégorgement à la volée*, which involves expelling the sediment without freezing it, is rarely used nowadays, though a highly traditional house like Salon still disgorges this way and it is a wonderful sight to see how they manage it by bringing the bottle to an upright position in a split second after the cork has been removed, thus preventing little more than the deposit from escaping.

However, a certain amount of wine is lost during *dégorgement* and to compensate for this, an equal amount of *liqueur de dosage*, a solution of cane sugar and still champagne, is added to the bottle. The sugar content of the liqueur will determine the wine's style and relative sweetness.

Dosage-adding machine at Louis Roederer

Corking machine at Louis Roederer

Hand-labelling at Champagne Palmer

Champagne Styles

THE ADDITION OF varying percentages of liqueur listed below broadly results in the following styles.

▌ **extra brut/brut intégral/brut zéro:** in these rare instances, no liqueur is added, the topping-up being done with the equivalent quantity of the same wine. The result is bone-dry champagne. Laurent-Perrier and Jacques Selosse are the best exponents

▌ **brut:** 1 percent liqueur is added, producing dry and classic champagne. The best cuvées are always reserved for the *brut*

▌ **extra-sec:** 1–3 percent liqueur produces a dry to medium dry champagne

▌ **demi-sec:** 3–5 percent liqueur is added, making a medium-sweet champagne

▌ **doux:** adding 8–15 percent liqueur makes a definitely sweet, dessert-style wine.

The Appreciation
═ *of Champagne* ═

THE SOUND OF POPPING CORKS and bursting bubbles are part of the magic of champagne, but its appearance, smell, and taste are a better guide to quality. Start your appraisal with the eyes, as the visual impression of the wine is an important signpost both

The Color of Champagne

A CHAMPAGNE SHOULD always be completely clear and ideally star-bright, so one which is cloudy or hazy has a definite fault. Most champagnes are yellow in color, spanning a range of hues from lemon and straw through primrose and buttermilk to gold and even bronze. A green tint can be an exciting sign of the wine's health and vitality; a brown tinge rings alarm bells, for it usually indicates that the champagne is past its best.

to its likely character and stage of maturity. Once the cork has been removed, pour a little champagne into a clear tulip-shaped glass to a level roughly 2 inches above the stem. Then look at the froth which dances on top of the wine; it should be snow-white. Now hold the glass by the stem and tilt it at an angle of 45 degrees against a white background, say a tablecloth or a sheet of paper, and study the wine's general appearance and color.

1 Straw yellow Pinot Meunier champagne
2 Full straw color: high percent of Pinot Noir
3 Deeper gold tints: wood-aged champagne
4 Delicate salmon pink: less red wine used in blend
5 Strong rosé pink: higher proportion of black grapes used by skin contact method

6 Older rosé (1985 vintage) with evolved shades of copper in the pink
7 Deep old gold of fully mature (16-year-old) Chardonnay from Le Mesnil
8 Vital lemon/straw yellow with green tints: a younger Blanc de Blancs champagne

Next study the bubbles (*mousse*) against a clear natural light. They should be uniform in shape, lively, and flow in a persistent stream toward the surface of the wine; Experts differ about the ideal size of the bubbles. Most Champenois say that the smaller the bubbles, the better the champagne, but large bubbles are not necessarily the sign of an inferior wine – your palate is a better judge.

Smell and Taste

More important is the smell of champagne. The nose is the most sensitive organ used when tasting wine; in fact, the sense of smell is so tightly linked with the sense of taste that the palate often confirms the sensations experienced by the nose. Hold the glass firmly by the stem and give it a good twirl to release the full aroma of the wine. Then put your nose into the glass and take several short sniffs rather than one long one, as the nose tires very easily, particularly with a sparkling wine. Note your impression – is the champagne's scent balanced and inviting?

Also consider that, just as color can indicate the age of champagne, so may smell. Young champagnes release the primary fruit flavors of the grapes from which they were made. Chardonnay smells floral and incisive, Pinot Noir fruity and well defined, Pinot Meunier spicy, soft, and often akin to fresh-baked bread. A typical non-vintage champagne is usually a blend of all three grapes, but if any one of these is dominant it will pervade the first aromas of the wine. Then there are the secondary aromas, which are essentially the smells of fermentation. Those rare champagnes that are fermented in wooden barrels often have an extracted, slightly bitter aroma. But with age, these special champagnes develop a lovely, toasty, scent. A fully mature champagne (six to ten years old) will have more complex aromas (the *bouquet*). Their smell is more vinous, less fruity than in a young wine, and in a mature champagne give a whiff of old yeasts which comes from long aging on the cork. This "autolycized" yeasty character adds complexity, but it should never mask the champagne's purity and clarity of expression.

And so to the most important test, the impact of the champagne on the palate, and its texture in the mouth.

Tasting Champagne

Appraising the appearance

Nosing the champagne

Tasting the champagne

Take a large sip, and, drawing air over the champagne (the attendant gurgling sound is optional), swill it round so that it reaches all parts of your mouth. This is a comic sight but it allows the tongue to appreciate fully the four basic sensations of sweetness (at the tongue's tip), acidity (at the sides), saltiness and bitterness (at the back). The first impression should be of cleanness of flavor and purity of fruit. The "clean" aspect is an essential characteristic, and as for the fruit, is it fresh and distinctive and does it hint at a Pinot or Chardonnay flavor?

A slight prickly sensation should impinge on the mouth and throat; the bubbles should agitate the oral membranes. Then the palate should register, in Jean-Claude Rouzaud's phrase, "champagne's restrained exuberance," fruity yet vinous, even and exquisitely balanced, but with a brisk hint of the chalk from which it came. Swallow and ask yourself if there is an aftertaste, for a great champagne leaves a distinctive taste at the back of the throat and lingers on the palate.

Learning from the Label

CHAMPAGNE IS THE ONLY quality French wine that does not show its controlled name of origin (*Appellation d'Origine Contrôlée*, or A.O.C.) status on the label. The name "Champagne" is in fact protected by law. However, the wine is subject to rigorous control and the label displays information that helps you decide which bottle to buy.

Remember these key points:

▌ Real champagne always carries the name "champagne" in prominent letters on the label, followed by the registered brand of the producer.

▌ Champagne invariably states its relative degree of dryness or sweetness, from bone-dry *Ultra Brut* to definitely sweet *Doux*, and where appropriate a particular style, such as *Blanc de Noirs* (made from black grapes only); *Blanc de Blancs* (made from white Chardonnay grapes exclusively).

▌ Vintage champagnes will display the appropriate date and in certain cases also the date of disgorging (*dégorgement*).

▌ The amount of wine in the bottle is declared: champagne bottles range in size from quarter bottles (18.7 centilitres) through standard bottles (75 centilitres) to the super giant Nebuchadnezzar (the equivalent of 20 standard bottles). Alcohol content is also stated as a percentage of liquid volume, usually about 12 percent.

▌ The town or village of the producer, and the country of origin (France), are displayed on the lower half.

▌ The most interesting item of information appears in tiny letters at the base of the label. This is the professional registration code devised in 1990 by the Comité Inter-professionel du Vin de Champagne (C.I.V.C.). The first two letters denote the type of champagne producer: N.M. (Negociant-Manipulant); R.M. (Récoltant-Manipulant); C.M. (Coopérative-Manipulant); S.R. (Société de Récoltant); R.C. (Récoltant-Cooperateur); M.A. (Marque d'Acheteur). (The different types of producer are defined in the **Glossary**.)

Date of the vintage
(1979 – an
exceptional year)

Name of the wine
(champagne)

Name of the brand
(the house that
made the
champagne)

Date of
dégorgement
(disgorging)

Producer's town
and country of
origin

Name of the
particular cuvée
(blend)

Alcohol content
(% by liquid
volume)

Bottle size

Professional Registration Code:
(denotes producer is a
négociant-manipulant)

Style – very dry

M.A. or *Marque d'Acheteur* loosely means "Buyer's Own Brand." Widely used by British wine merchants and supermarkets requiring their own label rather than that of the producer who makes the champagne for them.

How to Open a Bottle of Champagne

The pop as the cork is removed too abruptly heralds the discharge of a large quantity of the carbonic gas inside the bottle. It is much better that the fizz should be released gently through the wine in the glass.

Untwisting the wire muzzle

Easing the cork out of the bottle – forefinger curled over the cork

Here is the sequence you should follow:

▮ Have a glass nearby in case the removal of the cork is mishandled and the wine gushes out of the bottle.

▮ Cut off the foil surrounding the cork and untwist and remove the wire muzzle.

▮ Place the chilled bottle on a table or a flat surface. Grasp the bottle firmly in one hand, hold the cork with the other, with the thumb firmly placed on top of the cork and the other fingers around the neck of the bottle.

▮ Ease the cork out of the bottle, working it backward, forward, and upward with your thumbs, or you can work the cork with one hand while turning the bottle with the other. As soon as the cork starts to give, it is essential that the bottle should be tilted at an angle and the palm of one hand act as a brake, to prevent the cork from shooting out: when properly executed it should come off with a quiet sigh. If you have weak wrists, you can use special champagne tweezers to extract the cork.

Serving Champagne

An ice bucket for quick chilling should be half full of water, as well as ice

Serving champagne with panache is not easy. To remove the cork quietly, to cool the wine to the right temperature, and to pour it out without spraying your guests all involve dexterity, concentration, and a little practice.

CHILLING THE WINE

Champagne should be gently chilled rather than brutally iced, as it is impossible to appreciate the flavor of a frozen wine opened at 32°F. Serve champagne at a temperature of between 43 and 48°F since within this range not only are the smell and taste of champagne at their best, but the fizz inside the bottle is reduced to about one atmosphere of pressure, thus removing the danger of the effervescent wine gushing out of the bottle when the cork is removed. So either put the bottle of champagne in the refrigerator (*not* the freezer) for about one hour, setting the temperature at 43°F, or place the wine in an ice-bucket, half filled with ice, half with water, for 20 minutes or so.

These pointers are, of course, a rough rule of thumb which

should be adapted to the individual wine and the conditions in which it has been stored. An old vintage champagne usually needs less chilling than a young non-vintage one, and if you live in a small centrally heated apartment you should chill the champagne a little bit longer. You can store champagne in the refrigerator for 48 hours, but do not leave it there much longer because the cold will have a deadening effect on the wine's sparkle and flavor.

CHAMPAGNE ETIQUETTE

Before serving the champagne to your guests, pour a small amount into a glass, then smell and taste it to check there is no "corked" or moldy flavor. "Corked" champagne is much more

Champagne Glasses

GOOD CHAMPAGNE deserves good glasses, yet in the past their shape has often been contorted to satisfy the whim of fashion. The broad-topped champagned *coupe*, which was hugely popular in France from the time of the *Belle Epoque* until well into the 1960s, is in fact a useless glass for champagne, because the expensively produced bubbles go flat very quickly. The best all-purpose glass for both fine, sparkling, and still wines is a thin, tulip-shaped one, which tapers at the top to catch the full aromas of the wine. But the tulip is not special to champagne. One glass that is, the champagne *flute*, is very fashionable just now. The *flute*, with its slim, elongated shape, is very elegant, but until recently it was not an ideal glass for tasting champagne, since as Thomas Matthews of *The Wine Spectator* has pointed out, the narrow cylindrical shape of the classic *flute* encourages the wine to foam up rapidly, making appreciation of its qualities difficult.

The innovative Austrian glass designer, Georg Riedal, has responded to Matthews' criticism by developing a very good and relatively affordable flute called the *Prestige Cuvée* glass. In Riedal's words, "its wider opening and slightly curved bowl help deliver a much more intense

common than it used to be, so if you suspect that this is the case, stopper the wine at once and return it to the store where you bought it, together with the champagne cork. After extraction, the cork usually expands to a mushroom shape, but sometimes it remains peg-shaped: this is not necessarily the sign that the champagne is out of condition; it could mean that the wine is quite old or that it has been stored indifferently.

Once you are satisfied that the champagne is in good condition, fill the glasses, making sure that they are no more than two-thirds full so that the wine aromas may be appreciated without spilling the champagne. It's also a good idea to wrap the neck of the bottle with a napkin to prevent icy drops of wine dropping on to the shoulders of your guests, especially if they are glamorous women wearing scant little designer numbers from Dior.

bouquet and fuller body." As the champagne glass both for serious tasting and for aesthetic appeal on the dinner table, it is as good a one as you will find, costing about $16 a glass.

Good champagne glasses do not like dishwashers: quite apart from the danger of breakage, any trace of detergent or so-called "rinse" agent often leaves an industrial smell and even more frequently kills the sparkle of champagne.

Always hand-wash the glasses and rinse them thoroughly in warm water before drying and polishing them with a newly ironed tea-towel.

Classic tulip-shaped glass

Standard-sized flute

Large-size champagne flute

KEEPING AN OPENED BOTTLE OF CHAMPAGNE

Most people believe that a bottle of champagne has to be consumed at one sitting, as its sparkle goes flat very quickly. This is seldom true, for if you put an ordinary wine cork into a partially consumed bottle of champagne and return it to the refrigerator, it should remain in excellent form for 24 hours. And if you use a simple lever stopper, costing little more than $1, the champagne should retain its fizz for sevral days. In researching this book, which involved the sampling of hundreds of champagnes, I was amazed at just how long their sparkle lived when the wines were kept properly stoppered and chilled.

Pouring: the glass should be only half to two-thirds full to fully appreciate the aromas

Selection of champagne stoppers for storing partially consumed bottles of champagne

Champagne Bottle Sizes

Champagne is bottled in ten different sizes. However, only the half-bottle, bottle, and magnum are always released in the bottle in which they underwent the second fermentation. The Jeroboam and larger sizes are transferred under pressure (a technique called *transvasage*) from standard 75-centilitre/25.4-fluid ounce bottles, as are quarter-bottles. The huge bottles – the Salmanazar, Balthazar, and Nebuchadnezzar – are rarely made nowadays.

The different sizes with their total liquid volumes are:

QUARTER BOTTLE	18.7 cl/6.3 fluid ozs
HALF BOTTLE	37.5 cl/12.7 fluid ozs
BOTTLE	75 cl/25.4 fluid ozs
MAGNUM *(two bottles)*	1.5 litres/50.8 fluid ozs
JEROBOAM *(four bottles)*	3 litres/101.6 fluid ozs
REHOBOAM *(six bottles)*	4.5 litres/147 fluid ozs
METHUSELAH *(eight bottles)*	6 litres/196 fluid ozs
SALMANAZAR *(12 bottles)*	9 litres/304.8 fluid ozs
BALTHAZAR *(16 bottles)*	12 litres/406.4 fluid ozs
NEBUCHADNEZZAR *(20 bottles)*	15 litres/508 fluid ozs

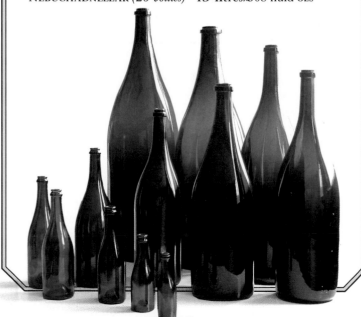

= *Champagne Vintage Chart* =

CHAMPAGNE IS AT HEART a blended wine, for in the cold marginal climate of north-east France the grapes do not ripen fully every year. So it is necessary to blend the wines of different vintages to create a palatable champagne. But maybe two or three times a decade, along comes an exceptional vintage which is good enough to drink on its own. Unfortunately there has been a recent trend in Champagne to declare a vintage too often and in unsuitable years. This guide points you to the true vintage years back to 1966 (the last year still widely available at auction).

The following quality code applies:

★★★ = outstanding year

★★ = true classic year

★   = decent year needing careful selection to find the best wines.

1993 Heavy rain in early September spoilt the prospects for a vintage year, though the early ripening Pinot Meunier grapes were of good quality.

1992 A mediocre year, diluted by rain, low in acidity and alcohol. Strictly for the blending vats.

1991 Overshadowed by the great 1990, actually not a bad year though not a classic. A few great houses like Bollinger may declare a vintage.

1990★★★ As elsewhere in Europe this will be a great long-vintage on a par with 1985 and 1982.

1989★★★ Another great vintage, voluptuous ripe wines which will mature quite quickly.

1988★★ A classic, well balanced year, firmer, drier, less showy than 1989 or 1990. Will keep well.

1987 Not in any sense a real vintage year, lacking complexity. Exceptions: Louise Pommery; Jacques Selosse *Cuvée d'Origine*.

1986 Although widely declared by many houses, decent though not a classic. Incipient rot in some grapes. Careful selection needed. Pol Roger's *Blanc de Chardonnay* is excellent.

1985★★★ A great, ripe, yet beautifully balanced year, but a small one. Outstanding bottles: Bollinger *Grande Année*, *Dom Pérignon*, Perrier-Jouet *Belle Epoque*.

1984 The least successful year of the decade. Avoid.

1983★★ Seriously undervalued by some critics, 1983 is a fine year with life-giving acidity. Excellent *Blanc de Blancs*, such as Charles Heidsieck *Cuvée des Millénaires* and *Dom Ruinart*.

1982★★★ Although unquestionably a very great, rich vintage, a few wines lack acidity. The best champagnes are wonderful, Krug a masterpiece.

1981★★ A small crop, some variation in quality, but the best wines like Krug, Roederer, and Bollinger have years of life in them.

1980 Declared by some houses, but shouldn't have been.

1979★★ A true vintage year, initially high in acidity, but showing beautifully now.

1978 Like 1980, declared by some houses but generally to be avoided.

1977 Poor. Roederer *Cristal* the only decent wine I know.

1976★★ Big majestic wines. The best, like Krug and Heidsieck *Diamant Bleu*, are magnificent. Some wines showing their age.

1975★★ For many years, wonderful champagnes of rare finesse. Quite a lot are past their best.

1974 Difficult year. Said to be a decent rosé vintage.

1973★★ Stylish, elegant wines. A few champagnes, if they have been well stored (like Krug), are still in their prime.

1972 Dreadful.

1971★★★ Long-lived wines of great class. Still full of life.

1970★★ Rich, generous wines which should be drunk quickly.

1969★★ High acidity has kept the best wines in sparkling condition. Salon *Le Mesnil* is superb.

1968 Very poor.

1967 Declared by some houses. Over the hill.

1966★★★ One of the greatest post-war vintages. Still drinking perfectly.

The best pre-1966 vintages: 1964, 1959, 1955, 1953, 1949, 1947.

Golden Oldies (Collectors' items): 1934, 1929, 1928, 1921, 1919, 1914, 1911, 1904.

DIRECTORY OF
MAJOR
Champagne
PRODUCERS

CHAMPAGNE IS THE ULTIMATE DRINK of celebration and conso-
lation. At moments of happiness and triumph there is
nothing quite like it. When times are hard it lifts your mood as
no other drink can. And yet behind the glamor is a remarkable
sparkling wine. This book aims to show why it is such a special
wine through the eyes of someone who has spent most of his
working life poking around the cellars of French wine growers.

The two directories of more than 100 champagne brands,
with detailed tasting notes of their currently available wines,
are the heart of the book. Champagne offers a huge range of
house styles and I have tried to focus on the distinguishing
features and wine-making philosophy of each firm as they
affect the flavor of its wines.

The Directory of Major Producers covers the major champagne brands widely available on export markets – the famous
grandes marques; champagnes from cooperatives, since these
often showed better in the glass, especially at non-vintage level,
than those of many famous firms; and, unusually, the best
champagnes from smaller growers. The perception of Champagne as dominated by 20 great firms is increasingly out of date.
Champagne is emerging from economic crisis. The industry is
in flux, and grower power is likely to assert itself in Champagne
in the late 1990s as it did in Burgundy in the 1980s.

The shorter directory which follows gives briefer profiles of
lesser-known champagne producers. Occasionally a well-known
producer who failed to provide sufficient information for a
major entry is profiled in the shorter directory.

Where I have made a critical comment about a champagne,
I have mentioned the date when I last tasted it, as wine is a
living thing and constantly changing. Where I have mentioned
a cuvée I have not tasted, I have said so.

INFORMATION BOXES

Information boxes give the location,
estimated yearly champagne production, and an overall 1-, 2- or 3-
star quality rating for each champagne house. A dish may be listed
that goes with the house's champagne style. Separate "Styles" boxes
list recommended cuvées.

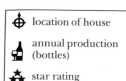

location of house

annual production
(bottles)

star rating

recommended
dish

HENRI ABELÉ

---

*Established in 1757, Henri Abelé is the third oldest
champagne house still trading and one with an
interesting history closely linked with innovations in
champagne-making.*

*I*n 1834, Auguste Ruinart de Brimont, great-nephew of
the founder, teamed up with Antoine Muller, former *chef de
caves* at Veuve Clicquot, who had helped the Widow Clicquot
develop the technique of *remuage*. Fifty years later, in 1884,
dégorgement à la glace, the method of disgorging now used
throughout the champagne industry, was invented in the
Abelé cellars. In 1942, control of the firm passed to the Com-
pagnie Française des Grands Vins, and in 1985 the firm was
purchased by Freixenet, the giant producers of Cava sparkling
wine. José Ferrer Sala, head of Freixenet, after tasting Henri
Abelé champagne for the first time, refused to buy a bottle.
Was he disappointed? Underwhelmed? Not a bit. Señor Ferrer
liked the wine so much that he decided to buy the company.

The style of the Abelé champagnes is reputedly dry, delicate
and floral. That is certainly true of the non-vintage *Cuvée
Sourire de Reims*, so named after the guardian angel of Reims
Cathedral, who grins at you from the label. It is an excellent,
consistent wine, light gold in color, with tiny bubbles, its flowery
yet mellow character coming from an unusual composition for
a non-vintage cuvée – up to 60 percent Chardonnay, 30 percent Pinot Meunier, and 10 percent Pinot Noir – and quite a
longer aging period in the bottle, I would guess, than the

Sourire de Reims N.V. *Grande Marque Impériale 1982*

modest two to two-and-a-half years claimed for it by the house. The non-vintage *Rosé Brut* is less subtle but full of flavor; pink-colored with a copper tinge, its zesty style may be due to the skin contact method used to partially color the champagne; it finishes with a slightly carmelized note, however, that for me militates against finesse. The vintage wines are a bit uneven in quality. Predominantly Pinot Noir, the 1982 *Grande Marque Impériale* seems to be losing its fruit, tastes low in acidity, and by the House's own admission is less successful than the 1976 and the 1975 vintages. The 1983 *Grande Marque Impériale* is better than the 1982, with crisper definition of flavor and a better fruit-to-acid balance. In a different league is the *Blanc de Blancs Réserve du Repas*, a wine made only in great years. The 1983 is a beauty, impeccably dry but with the mellow creamy perfection of flavor that comes from top-notch flight Chardonnay champagne which is allowed to mature properly for a decade.

⊕ Reims

 500,000 bottles

★ good quality

STYLES
NON-VINTAGE
SOURIRE DE REIMS
ROSÉ
ROSÉ BRUT
VINTAGE
GRANDE MARQUE IMPÉRIALE (1982, 1983)
PRESTIGE
BLANC DE BLANCS, RÉSERVE DU REPAS (1983)

Sourire de Reims N.V. ▶

MICHEL ARNOULD

Michel Arnould and his son Patrick are typical of Champagne growers whose grand cru grapes are much in demand for the blends of the grandes marques.

*A*rnould still grows for Bollinger, although he also now makes and markets his champagnes under the Arnould label from his 30 acres of superbly sited vineyards at Verzenay. Arnould champagnes are distinguished from other growers' *monocrus* by their breed, balance, and creamy texture. Their wines are every bit as good as the non-vintage cuvées of the great houses and they always score very highly in blind tastings.

The *Brut* is a true *Blanc de Noirs* (100 percent Pinot Noir) and a blend of wines from two vintages, aged for three years in the bottle, and ready to drink. It shows gorgeous, creamy fruit, plenty of body, but is never over-extracted or heavy in flavor; it is very compelling and you invariably want a second, third, and fourth glass – always the sign of a really good champagne

⊕ Verzenay

🍾 80,000 bottles

★★ excellent quality

🍽 tarte tatin (*Demi-Sec*), sea-bass with fennel

Grand Cru Brut

for all occasions. The *Demi-Sec* is identical in composition to the *Brut*, except it has a higher *dosage* and is obviously sweeter; try it with tarte tatin, the glorious French upside-down apple tart. *Brut Réserve*, definitely dry, is blended from two-thirds Pinot Noir and one-third Chardonnary, the latter giving a "lift" and sharp definition to this top cuvée, its touch of austerity making it a wine for special-occasion fish dishes, such as roasted sea-bass with fennel.

An Arnould champagne would be a desert island wine of my choice, encouraging me to throw away the loaded revolver and wait for the sight of the rescue ship on the far horizon.

Pinot Noir grapes

STYLES
NON-VINTAGE
GRAND CRU BRUT
GRAND CRU DEMI-SEC
PRESTIGE
GRAND CRU BRUT RÉSERVE

Grand Cru Brut: a Blanc de Noirs ▶

AYALA

*Ayala vintage wines are discreet champagnes for those
who like delicacy rather than power.*

A famous champagne name in the past, Ayala is rather out of fashion these days. The firm was founded in 1860 by Edmond d'Ayala, the son of a Colombian diplomat, who married Gabrielle d'Albrecht, niece of the Vicomte de Mareuil. Part of Gabrielle's dowry was a Mareuil vineyard, rated at 99 percent on the *échelle de cru*, which this independent *grande marque* house still owns.

Ayala champagnes are pale in color, light-bodied, and definitely dry. In my experience the non-vintage *Brut* is very variable in quality; one bottle sampled in London in November 1993 was green, lean, and mean, a second tasted in France two months later was subtle and fine. The *Brut Rosé* (100 percent Pinot Noir) is straightforward, soft, and round, although its flavor disappears quickly in the mouth.

The vintage wines are in a different league. The 1985 is a real success in an outstanding year, the lingering taste of high-class Pinot Noir (70 percent of the grape mix) making this a

⊕ Ay

🍾 800,000 bottles

★ good quality

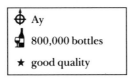

Brut Rosé

delicious wine and one to search out. The 1985 *Blanc de Blancs* does not lack class but it needs keeping until 1995 to soften its mouth-puckering acidity. The prestige *Grande Cuvée*, currently the 1985 soon to be joined by the 1988, is also a bit young to drink but it has a latent complexity of nutty Chardonnay-dominated flavors which will eventually blossom if you have the time, space, and money to age this wine.

The vineyard at Ay

STYLES

NON-VINTAGE
BRUT

ROSÉ
BRUT ROSÉ

VINTAGE
BLANC DE BLANCS
(1985)

PRESTIGE
GRANDE CUVÉE
(1985, 1988)

Brut Rosé: Pinot Noir ▶

BARANCOURT

*In the stratified champagne world of grandees and
peasant farmers, Barancourt's is a rare modern tale of
little guys becoming big shots.*

*I*n 1966 three Bouzy growers – Brice, Martin, and Tritant
– joined forces to make and market champagne, later re-
suscitating the famous name Barancourt for their brand. During the 1970s the partners bought further *grand cru* vineyards,
especially in Bouzy, Cramant, and in the Aube. They now
grow all three champagne grapes in a *domaine* totalling nearly
247 acres. Much of their production, including all the Pinot
Meunier, is sold to other houses, but wines on the Barancourt
label are made from *grand cru* Pinot Noir and Chardonnay.
The Barancourt style is difficult to pinpoint, since the range is
wide. You could say these are champagne-makers' champagnes,
with a firm, strong character of the *crus* from which they come.
They are anything but showy, need an awful lot of aging, and
maybe lack an easy charm.

Brut Réserve

Blanc de Blancs

*Grand Cru Bouzy
Brut Rosé 1985*

*Grand Cru Bouzy
Brut 1985*

The non-vintage *Brut Réserve* is a well-structured wine (80 percent Pinot Noir) but with a yeasty character which subdues the fruit. The non-vintage *Blanc de Blancs* is light and well balanced, yet this is an austere, very young-tasting wine, its potential Chardonnary flavors only half realized in the glass (tasted January 1994). The non-vintage *Brut Rosé is* full-colored and fruity and a much better value than the expensive, rather heavy and autolytic 1985 *Grand Cru Rosé*. The vintage wines, currently the 1985s, are decent champagnes – the monocrus *Bouzy* and *Cramant* are worth trying – but they all need to age longer. The Barancourt *Bouzy Rouge*, a still Coteaux Champenois wine, can be delicious in great years like 1982 and 1985. The 1990 will be spectacular. Barancourt was sold to Vranken-Lafitte in 1994.

 Bouzy

550,000 bottles

★ good quality

STYLES

NON-VINTAGE
BRUT RÉSERVE
BLANC DE BLANCS

ROSÉ
BRUT ROSÉ

VINTAGE
BRUT (1985)
GRAND CRU
CRAMANT BRUT (1985)
GRAND CRU
BOUZY BRUT
BOUZY ROUGE,
COTEAUX CHAMPENOIS
(recommended vintages
1982, 1985)

PRESTIGE
GRANDE CUVÉE
(1985, 1988)

Brut Réserve N.V. ▶

BEAUMET

Founded at Pierry in 1878, Beaumet is now owned by
Jacques Trouillard and operates from splendid premises
in Epernay's beautiful Park Malakoff.

he company owns 198 acres of vineyards both on the Côte des Blancs and above the Marne, the jewels being the 74 acres of *grand cru* Chardonnay at Avize, Cramant, and Chouilly. So it is not surprising that by far the best wine here is the *Cuvée Malakoff Blanc de Blancs*, which is aged for a minimum of seven years; both the 1982 and 1985 are first-rate 100 percent Chardonnay champagnes, gold-green in color, nutty, and creamy, yet fine-drawn and long. Overshadowed by the Malakoff, the others in the range are decent champagnes

Rosé 1981

Brut 1981

Cuvée Malakoff

Blanc de Noirs 1981

Blanc de Blancs N.V.

(usually with a significant percentage of Pinot Meunier) for those who like flavor rather than finesse. The non-vintage *Brut* makes easy drinking; the *Rosé Brut* is dark pink with a black grape fruitiness; and both the vintage-dated *Blanc de Noirs* and the 1985 *Brut* are mouth-filling and mellow. Beaumet is better known in the United States and Great Britain than in France.

Vineyards at Cramant on the Côte des Blancs

⊕ Epernay

🍾 1.5 million bottles

★ good quality

STYLES

NON-VINTAGE

BRUT

ROSÉ

BRUT ROSÉ

VINTAGE

BLANC DE NOIRS (1985)

BRUT (1985)

PRESTIGE

CUVÉE MALAKOFF
BLANC DE BLANCS
(recommended vintages
1985, 1982, 1981, 1979)

Blanc de Blancs ▶

BEAUMONT
DES CRAYÈRES

*A champagne cooperative created in 1955, now with 200
member-growers. For quality and value for the money,
Beaumont des Crayères champagnes are hard to beat.*

*B*eaumont des Crayères is unusual in that the size of its
average member's vineyard is just 1¼ acres. This small-
ness of scale allows for a very strict control over the maturity of
the grapes, which are then vinified with meticulous care in a
modern winery by Jean-Paul Bertus, one of the best *chefs de
caves* in Champagne.

The finesse and vivid flavors of Beaumont's champagnes
have won press plaudits, notably from the authoritative *Guide
Hachette* in France and the influential *Wine Spectator* in North
America. The non-vintage *Cuvée Réserve Brut* is made largely
from Pinot Meunier (50 percent) which explains its lovely fruity
aroma tinged with the scent of wild mushrooms; the palate is
supple and mouth-filling, the finish long and persistent – an
exciting champagne for a very reasonable price. *Cuvée Rosé
Privilège*, again predominantly Pinot Meunier, has spicy fruit,

Rosé Privilège

Cuvée de Réserve

Cuvée Spéciale Nostalgie 1985

though to my taste it is a little chunky and obvious. *Cuvée de Prestige*, made from roughly equal parts of the three classic champagne grapes, is a powerful wine with enough flavor to match roast guinea fowl. *Cuvée Spéciale Nostalgie Millésimé* 1985 (shortly to be replaced by the 1987) is a pure Chardonnay champagne, its incisive acidity and mineral flavor reflecting the chalky soil from which it came.

Old Chardonnay Vines

 Mardeuil

240,000 bottles

★★ excellent quality

roast guinea fowl

STYLES

NON-VINTAGE

CUVÉE RÉSERVE BRUT

ROSÉ

CUVÉE ROSÉ PRIVILÈGE

PRESTIGE

CUVÉE DE PRESTIGE

CUVÉE SPÉCIALE NOSTALGIE (1985)

Cuvée Réserve Brut ▶

ALBERT BEERENS

A small Aube grower, Beerens cultivates a vineyard of 15 acres, planted with 80 percent Pinot Noir, about 20 percent Chardonnay, and no Pinot Meunier.

Beerens makes just two champagnes for the export market. The very consistent *Brut* has a vibrant straw-gold color, a lively yet subtle *mousse,* and a round balanced flavor that comes from three or four years of aging before sale. The *Brut Rosé* is excellent. Salmon-pink in color, racy, with a beautifully pure definition of fruit flavors, it is made with a good proportion of Chardonnay to which about 7 percent still red Champenois wine is added. An unbeatable partner for a simply grilled lobster if you are in the mood for champagne. The exceptional quality of these wines comes from the company's low-yielding vines.

⊕ Bar-sur-Aube

🍾 35,000 bottles

★★ excellent quality

🍴 grilled lobster

STYLES
NON-VINTAGE
BRUT
ROSÉ
BRUT ROSÉ

Brut Réserve ▶

PAUL BERTHELOT

This serious little champagne house, established for 100 years, uses 95 percent of its own grapes from its vineyards around Ay.

The two brothers who run the firm are reluctant to give hard information about themselves, hence the shortness of this entry. However, the *Brut Réserve* is an excellent non-vintage champagne which handily bests many widely publicized brands. Its shimmering straw-gold color, tiny bubbles, and creamy long flavor suggest a lot of high-class Pinot Noir grapes are used in the blend. Other offerings include a fruity, well-balanced *Rosé Brut* and the prestige *Cuvée du Centenaire* 1983 (not tasted). Berthelot champagnes have a niche in the cost-conscious British market – no surprise, for they feature a good ratio of quality to price.

⊕	Dizy
🍾	150,000 bottles
★	good quality

STYLES

NON-VINTAGE
BRUT RÉSERVE

ROSÉ
ROSÉ BRUT

PRESTIGE
CUVÉE DU CENTENAIRE
(1983)

Cuvée de Centenaire 1983 ▶

BILLECART-SALMON

This small family-run grande marque house, founded in 1818, is now one of the most innovative in wine-making techniques.

The house was founded by Nicolas-François Billecart, who had married a Mlle. Salmon. Billecart quickly opened up markets around the world for his wines, but in 1830 disaster struck when an incompetent American agent, Mr. Meyer of New York, lost the firm 100,000 gold francs (the equivalent of $30 million in today's money). The family went into a commercial sleep for nearly 100 years, until 1926, when Charles Roland-Billecart put the firm's affairs on a sound commercial basis by selling the family vineyards to finance the increased champagne sales he had achieved since the end of the First World War. His grandson, François Roland-Billecart, now effectively runs the company, quietly expanding production year by year without compromising its reputation for quality.

Billecart looks for finesse as a house style, yet the delicacy of these champagnes is deceptive for they also have exceptional aging potential. This is achieved, say the Billecarts, by a special fermentation technique. After the first clarification process (*débourbage*), a second one is induced by chilling the must down to about 41°F, which acts as a filtration and eliminates most of the natural yeasts. The temperature is then raised to about 52–

Maison Billecart-Salmon in Mareuil-sur-Ay

59°F, and fermentation proceeds slowly for about 21 days. Oxidation of the must is entirely avoided. As proof that these champagnes do indeed live long distinguished lives, a 1959 Billecart was still vigorously alive in 1991.

The outstanding non-vintage *Brut*, based on Pinot Noir, is firm and well structured, the vintage *Blanc de Blancs* (1985 is an excellent year), made from prime Chardonnay grapes from Cramant, Avize, and Le-Mesnil-sur-Oger, is fine and subtle; so is the *Brut Rosé*, its pale salmon color explained by the addition of a smaller amount of red wine to the blend than usual. The Prestige *Cuvée Columbus* made from the 1986, 1985, and 1979 vintages, is magnificent.

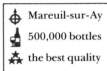

- ⊕ Mareuil-sur-Ay
- 500,000 bottles
- ✸ the best quality
- ¡O¡ Beaufort cheese

Vintage 1985

Blanc de Blancs 1985

Brut Rosé ▶

STYLES

NON-VINTAGE	VINTAGE
BRUT	CUVÉE NICOLAS FRANÇOIS BILLECART (1986)
ROSÉ	BLANC DE BLANCS (1985) (1982 also available)
BRUT ROSÉ	PRESTIGE
	CUVÉE COLUMBUS

Brut 1982

Cuvée N.F. Billecart Brut 1986

Brut Rosé

◀ *Brut*

HENRI BILLIOT

*Henri Billiot makes a tiny amount of superlative
champagne from his 5 acres of grand cru Pinot Noir
vines at Ambonnay.*

The *Cuvée de Réserve* has a depth of flavor
and sinewy power that stopped me in my tracks
when I tasted it in December 1993. The *Cuvée
Réserve Rosé* has stunning quality too; close your
eyes and you might be drinking great burgundy
with bubbles. The wines are on strict allocation,
the lion's share of which goes to Bibendum Wine
Ltd. of London.

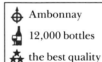

BRUT   1989

CHAMPAGNE

H. BILLIOT FILS

PROPRIÉTAIRES · RÉCOLTANTS

GRAND CRU 100%   à AMBONNAY
· (MARNE)

75 cl   Élaboré par H. BILLIOT Fils Ambonnay 51150 . France   L-994   12% vol.

Brut Rosé 1989

⊕ Ambonnay

🍾 12,000 bottles

✸ the best quality

STYLES

CUVÉE DE RÉSERVE

ROSÉ

CUVÉE DE RÉSERVE
ROSÉ

Cuvée Laetitia ▶

H. BLIN & CO.

For decent no-frills champagnes, better in blind tastings than some also-ran grandes marques, *this is a label to remember.*

"*H*. Blin & Co." is the brand label of a Marne Valley cooperative established at Vincelles in 1947. Its members cultivate 222 acres of mainly Pinot Meunier grapes which are pressed in an ultra-modern winery. The *Brut Tradition* is made entirely from black grapes (80 percent Pinot Meunier) and is a round, fruity champagne with mocha-like aromas. Pinot Meunier drives the heady red fruit flavors of the *Rosé*.

Brut 1986

⊕	Vincelles
🍾	500,000 bottles
★	good quality

STYLES
NON-VINTAGE
BRUT TRADITION
ROSÉ
BRUT ROSÉ

Brut Tradition ▶

BOIZEL

The only woman who currently heads a champagne house is Evelyn Roques-Boizel, who took charge of this family-owned company in 1984.

The champagne trade is notable for resourceful women who have led some of the most famous houses. Evelyn Roques-Boizel continues that tradition. She became head of Boizel 150 years after it was founded by Auguste Boizel, her great-grandfather, and immediately invested in a new *cuverie* on Epernay's rue de Bernon. In the last 10 years she has more than doubled annual production to one million bottles. Boizel owns no vines, but buys grapes from growers in 51 villages.

Boizel champagnes are briskly effervescent and clean-tasting; they sell for sensible prices, but lack the class and complexity of those from the best houses. *Brut Réserve* (non-

The maison Boizel in Epernay

vintage), dominated by Pinot Noir (55 percent), is a simple
fruity wine; it is hard to believe, however, that it has much
bottle age, for its aroma is green and reminiscent of apples.
Brut Rosé is a much better wine, limpid pale pink with an invigorating racy flavor; it won the "Coup de Coeur" in the
1989 *Guide Hachette. Brut Blanc de Blancs* (not
tasted) was relaunched in 1984 to celebrate
the firm's 150th anniversary; its label, a reproduction of a Second Empire one, is a collector's item. *Grand Vintage* 1986 has good
fizz, is lemon-gold in color, and refined yet
vigorous.

Brut Réserve

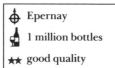

⊕ Epernay

🍾 1 million bottles

★★ good quality

STYLES
NON-VINTAGE
BRUT RÉSERVE
BRUT BLANC DE BLANCS
ROSÉ
BRUT ROSÉ
VINTAGE
GRAND VINTAGE (1986)
PRESTIGE
"JOYAU DE FRANCE"

Brut 1986 ▶

BOLLINGER

Bollinger is one of the greats of champagne, a true
grande marque *with a very proud tradition dating back*
to the 15th century, when the de Villermont family first
acquired vineyards in Cuis, on the Côte des Blancs.

*I*ts attachment to the land has stood Bollinger in good stead over the past five centuries and is particularly important today. The firm owns 346 acres of vineyards, mainly in prime sites around Ay on the Montagne de Reims, and these supply 70 percent of its needs, allowing Bollinger to ensure an enviable continuity of style and quality.

The house was founded in 1829 by Joseph Bollinger, a native of Württemberg, Germany, and Paul Renaudin, a Champenois. Renaudin soon left the firm, but his name remained on the label until the 1960s. Joseph Bollinger married a de Villermont, continued to expand the business, and in 1865 was one of the first merchants to ship champagne to

Bollinger headquarters in Ay

England. This was an extremely dry champagne of low *dosage* in contrast to most other houses' champagnes, which were then sweet. Bollinger became the favorite champagne of the Prince of Wales, the future King Edward VII. In 1870 Joseph Bollinger exported his first shipment to the United States, where later the brand was widely distributed by Julius Wile, the great New York wine merchant, from just before Prohibition until 1988.

During the Second World War, the direction of the firm passed to the remarkable Madame Lily Bollinger on the death of her husband Jacques, grandson of Joseph. She faced three years' occupation by the Germans. With no gasoline available, she toured the family vineyards on foot and bicycle. Despite a totally depleted labor force, she continued to produce and sell champagne, and with one remaining servant, slept in the Bollinger cellars during Allied bombardments, including the American raid of August 10, 1944, which destroyed one-third of Ay. After the war, she acquired prime vineyards in Ay, Grauves, Bisseuil, and Champvoisy, bringing Bollinger's holdings to their current extent. Until well into her 70s, "Tante Lily", as she was known to her family, was a familiar sight in her tweeds, bicycling through the vineyards. Over nearly 40 years, she doubled Bollinger's sales to one million bottles a year.

On the death of Mme. Bollinger in 1977, her nephew Christian Bizot became President of the company. Bizot is a clear-headed and articulate man who combines commitment to the quality of Bollinger champagne with an unsentimental awareness of the confused consumer perception of champagne.

Madame Lily Bollinger

Acutely conscious of the severe criticisms of the quality of champagne at a time of increasing competition from quality sparkling wines, Bizot responded in 1991 by publishing the Bollinger *Charter of Ethics and Quality*. The *Charter* chronicles in meticulous detail the company's wine-making practices.

The most important of these is Bollinger's use of grapes of the highest quality. Of the firm's vineyards, 60 percent are classified as *grand cru* and 30 percent as *premier cru*. Bollinger keeps only the juice from the first pressings (the cuvée) and sells that from the second pressings to companies whose business is cheap champagne. The high quality of the must allows Bollinger to ferment its vintage wines in wooden casks. This gives the wines an inimitable robust style unlike those that have been fermented in stainless steel. Bollinger insists that a great champagne needs time on its lees (the by-product of fermentation) to develop personality and complexity. Non-vintage champagnes are aged for a minimum of three years (the legal minimum is 12 months), vintage wines for five, and deluxe vintage cuvées for eight.

The *Special Cuvée* (60 percent Pinot Noir, 25 percent Chardonnay and 15 percent Pinot Meunier) is a non-vintage wine which is fermented in

⊕ Ay

🍾 1.5 million bottles

★★ the best quality available

🍽 rosette of beef

Vieilles Vignes Françaises 1986 ▶

RD 1982

Grande Année 1985

Rosé 1985

Bollinger Special Cuvée

STYLES	
NON-VINTAGE	**PRESTIGE**
SPECIAL CUVÉE	ANNÉE RARE RD (1982)
VINTAGE	(older recommended vintage: 1975)
GRANDE ANNÉE (1985)	
ROSÉ (1985)	VIEILLES VIGNES FRANÇAISES (1985)

stainless steel to control the malolactic fermentation, a process which makes wine softer and rounder. *Special Cuvée* is a full-bodied, firm, and dry champagne with great Pinot Noir fruit and length of flavor on the palate; it is the sort of weighty fizz you only want a glass or two of before dinner.

The 1985 *Grande Année* (62 percent Pinot Noir, 35 percent Chardonnay, 3 percent Pinot Meunier) has a fine *mousse* of tiny bubbles, a deep flavor of *grand cru* Pinot Noir (tempered with the finesse of a higher proportion of Chardonnay), and incredible length on the palate. It will improve until 1998–2000. The 1982 *Année Rare* R.D. (recently disgorged) is left on its lees for three years more than *Grande Année* for a more developed style. The 1982 has a lovely smell of ripe, red fruit but a complex vinous (rather than fruity) flavor that lingers.

Bollinger champagnes come into their own with food.

BRICOUT

---

*Founded in 1820 and known until recently as Bricout &
Koch, this house produces wines correctly made from
mainly Chardonnay grapes in a clean, modern style.*

*I*n 1820 Charles Koch, a young German
from Heidelberg, went into the champagne
business in Avize. His sons became partners of
Arthur Bricout, a former wine maker for de
Venoge, who in the 1870s merged the two
family firms.

These champagnes were first popular in
Germany, but since 1979 and a big injection of
cash from the Racke group, their customer base
has been widened, especially to the restaurant
trade in France. The wines are now labelled
Bricout.

Carte D'Or Brut Prestige

Carte Noir Brut N.V.

Millésimé Brut 1985

Carte D'Or Brut Prestige ▶

You have to pick and choose to find the best cuvées. The big-selling *Carte Noir Brut* is lively, fruity, but young-tasting. The *Carte d'Or Brut Prestige* has much more class, with a predominant taste of ripe Chardonnay and a smooth mature finish. The 1985 *Élégance de Bricout* is everything its name implies, elegant lemony color, elegant fine-drawn flavor, and a flick of acidity to ensure it will improve in bottle for several years. The non-vintage *Rosé Brut* (80 percent Chardonnay) is very light in color and its taut dry style may not be to everyone's taste. The *Brut Millésimé* 1985 is one Bricout wine with a lot of Pinot Noir (60 percent), and although quite rich and round is not as exciting as the Chardonnay-based wines from this house.

⊕ Avize

2.8 million bottles

★ good quality

STYLES

NON-VINTAGE
CARTE NOIRE BRUT

VINTAGE
MILLÉSIMÉ BRUT (1985)

ROSÉ
ROSÉ BRUT

PRESTIGE
CARTE D'OR BRUT PRESTIGE

ÉLÉGANCE DE BRICOUT (1985)

◀ *Élégance de Bricout 1985*

CANARD-DUCHÊNE

A big producer of inexpensive champagnes with regular annual sales of 3 million bottles.

Canard-Duchêne, founded in 1868, is now overshadowed by Veuve Clicquot, which bought the company in 1978. The firm is none-theless a major supplier of champagne to the French market. The standard *Brut* is not recom-mended; tasted twice in November 1993 and February 1994, this wine had a suspiciously deep, tinted color and a coarse flavor on each occasion. The vintage wines, by contrast, are perfectly decent, though they are made in very small quantities. The *Patrimoine* 1988 has a pleasantly yeasty nose and is well balanced on the palate while the prestige *Cuvée Charles VII* is rich and voluptuous. More work please on the standard *Brut*, which as the flagship brand of a *grande marque* house is an embarrass-ment on current showing.

 Ludes

3 million bottles

★ average quality

STYLES·

NON-VINTAGE

BRUT

VINTAGE

PATRIMOINE (1988)

PRESTIGE

CUVÉE CHARLES VII

Patrimoine Brut 1985 ▶

A. CHARBAUT

—

Charbaut is a quality operation at all stages of champagne-making and a champagne house to watch.

This family firm was established in 1948, and is now run by René and Guy Charbaut, with Guy's son-in-law, Jean-Pierre Abiven. The company has seen a strong expansion in recent years. Today the family owns 144 acres of *premier cru* and *grand cru* vineyards, classified between 95 and 100 percent on the *échelle de cru*. The company also has an option to buy land in upstate New York, the long-term aim being to produce

Certificate Blanc de Blancs 1985

Brut Réserve

Blanc de Blancs

Rosé Brut

Millésime 1987

an American sparkling wine in a cold climate similar to that of Champagne.

The non-vintage *Brut Réserve* is made from a rigorous selection of wines from the Charbaut vineyards and is a blend of one-third Chardonnay and two-thirds Pinot Noir. A complex, elegant, yet deep-flavored champagne, its very distinctive style, particularly apparent in its winey aroma, comes from aging on the lees for four years before being disgorged. The non-vintage *Blanc de Blancs* is exceptional. Its delicate *mousse* and exquisite smell and taste is both refined and full of character. The 1985 *Certificate Blanc de Blancs* is a memorable rich and mellow wine made with the best ripe Chardonnay grapes in an outstanding year for *Blanc de Blancs* champagne. The *Vintage* 1985 *Cuvée*, on the couple of occasions I have drunk it, seemed closed and withdrawn (last tasted in December 1993) and probably should not be consumed before 1995.

⊕ Epernay

🍾 1.5 million bottles

★★ excellent quality

STYLES

NON-VINTAGE
BRUT RÉSERVE
BLANC DE BLANCS

ROSÉ
ROSÉ BRUT

VINTAGE
CERTIFICATE BLANC
DE BLANCS (1985)

---

*Certificate Blanc de Blancs
from the outstanding 1985
vintage* ▶

VEUVE CLICQUOT-PONSARDIN

*The fabled Nicole-Barbe Clicquot (née Ponsardin) was
the most gifted of the champagne widows. On the death of
her adored husband in 1806, this determined woman,
aged just 27, buried her grief by relaunching the family
firm as Veuve Clicquot-Ponsardin.*

Turning her back on the cost-conscious French and British merchants, Mme. Clicquot sought new customers for her champagnes in eastern Europe. She dispatched Heinrich Bohne, a brilliant salesman, to St. Petersburg, and in 1814 penetrated an Allied blockade to ship her 1811 vintage to the Russian court. Russia became a prime market which Clicquot was to dominate for the next 50 years. The widow was a great spotter of talent. Her *chef de caves*, Antoine Muller, perfected the technique of *remuage* in 1818, and Edouard Werlé, her business manager, saved her from pressing creditors by hocking his own assets when her firm's Paris bankers went into liquidation in 1828. The grateful Mme. Clicquot made Werlé a partner in the business, and it was he who established the brand on world markets. By the time of the widow's death at 89 in 1866, annual sales had reached three million bottles. The firm was also ably run for 50 years by Comte Bertrand de

Jacques Peters — Veuve Clicquot winemaker

Mun, a descendant of Werlé. Since the late 1970s, Clicquot has entered the impersonal world of acquisitions and mergers, gaining control of Canard-Duchêne champagne and merging with Joseph Henriot. The company is now part of the Louis Vuitton Vuitton-Moët-Hennessy (L.V.M.H.) conglomerate.

Veuve Clicquot owns one of the largest vineyards in Champagne, some 704 acres. This beautiful estate was essentially the work of the widow Clicquot and says a lot about her shrewdness. It is very evenly spread across the classic wine-growing districts and comprises a large number of *grands crus* such as Avize, Cramant, Oger, and Le Mesnil on the Côte des Blancs, and Ambonnay, Verzenay, and Bouzy on the Montagne de Reims. Yet these vineyards account for just one-third of the company's needs. Like most great houses with rock-solid reputations, Clicquot is an important buyer of Pinot Meunier grapes for its non-vintage cuvées.

Wine-making at Clicquot is thoroughly modern and all the wines are fermented in stainless steel vats of varying capacities depending on the provenance of the musts. No wood has been used since 1961. The style of the wines has changed in recent years, in my view for the better; although still deep-flavored and dominated by black grapes, they are fresher, and less oxidized than they used to be, with an emphasis on pure fruit definition. This has not been achieved at the expense of complexity, for an admirably high percentage of reserve wines is used in the blends, and the finished champagnes are given plenty of bottle age before sale. Joseph Henriot, head of Clicquot until 1994, and Jacques Peters, his

La Grande Dame Cuvée Prestige ▶

La Grande Dame 1985   *Brut Rosé 1983*

meticulous technical director, can take the lion's share of credit for this, although their decisions are always checked by a tasting committee of directors and managers.

The non-vintage *Brut* with its unmistakable yellow label is currently right back on form. Its ripe red fruits and spice flavor, shaped by the dominant Pinot Noir (56 percent), a good touch of Pinot Meunier (about 16 percent), and plenty of reserve wines; yet it is fresh and crisp, Chardonnay (28 percent) is the tempering hand. The Gold label *Vintage Réserve Brut* 1985 got my top mark at a tasting of *grande marque* champagnes from that great year organized by the Institute of British Masters of Wine in 1993; luscious yet lithe with a beautiful filbert bouquet. The prestige cuvée *La Grande Dame* is almost always among the best three or four luxury champagnes on the market; the 1985 is a masterpiece of mellow mouth-enveloping richness and faultless balance. The vintage-dated *Rosé* has its fans, although I am not among them.

STYLES

NON-VINTAGE
BRUT "YELLOW LABEL"

VINTAGE
RÉSERVE (1985)
VINTAGE-DATED ROSÉ

PRESTIGE
LA GRANDE DAME
(1985)

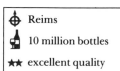

Reims

10 million bottles

★★ excellent quality

ANDRÉ CLOUET

*Clouet champagnes reflect the special character of their
exceptionally sited Pinot Noir vineyards, all rated at 100
percent on the échelle de cru.*

Their 22-acre estate on the best middle slopes of Bouzy
and Ambonnay is run by Pierre and Françoise Santz-Clouet,
a hardworking and open-minded couple. The house's ornate
ancien regime labels are no doubt a nostalgic tribute to the
founder of the estate, a printer to the royal court at Versailles
during the reign of Louis XV.

André Clouet Grand Cru Brut Réserve is a big rich Pinot Noir
champagne with a vinosity typical of Bouzy. Made from a
selection of the first pressings of the grapes (*tête de cuvée*), this
wine is matured for a long time on the lees before being disgorged, which accounts for its complexity and long persistent
finish. The *Grand Cru Rosé* is a typical grower's wine in the best
sense. Of rich heather-like color, the primary aromas of Pinot
Noir soar out of the glass; the bubbles are lively but the balance
of fruit and flavor in the mouth is excellent. The 1989 *Vintage
Grand Cru Brut* is an impressive effort in a very ripe year. The
flavor is round and mouth-filling, not clumsy or overblown,
thanks to good acidity.

Bouzy is famous for its red still wine made from 100 percent Pinot Noir. But to show at its best it needs a sunny year.
The 1988 vintage was one such year and the Clouets' example
is first-rate: the color is a vivid ruby, the nose redolent of
raspberries, the flavor succulent yet elegant. It is also a versatile
wine with food, good with pasta dishes, grilled fish, or cheese.

Grand Cru Rosé

```
┌─────────────────────────────────────────┐
│                 STYLES                   │
│                                          │
│   NON-VINTAGE              ROSÉ          │
│   GRAND CRU BRUT       GRAND CRU ROSÉ    │
│      RÉSERVE                              │
│                         VINTAGE          │
│              GRAND CRU BRUT (1989)       │
│              BOUZY ROUGE (1988)          │
└─────────────────────────────────────────┘
```

Grand Cru Brut 1989

Bouzy Rouge

 Bouzy

 60,000 bottles

★★ excellent quality

|O| Bouzy Rouge with creamy pasta, grilled fish, or cheese

◀ *Grand Cru Rosé (Pinot Noir)*

DE CASTELLANE

Founded in 1895 by a Provençal nobleman,
de Castellane has a grand past symbolized by its bizarre
crenellated tower which dominates the drab skyline
of Epernay.

*U*ntil the mid-1980s, the firm was one of the few to ferment a high percentage of its wines in large oak casks. Laurent-Perrier now has a controlling interest in the company, modern methods are being introduced, and the wines are rather lighter than they used to be.

Respected critics such as Robert Parker rate these champagnes highly, which puzzles me as I find them a very mixed bag. The Pinot Noir- and Meunier-dominated non-vintage *Brut Croix Rouge de Saint André*, which accounts for 70 percent of the firm's sales, is not overpriced but often tastes coarse and green with a higher than average *dosage*. The *Rosé Brut* is also nothing to get excited about. The *Vintage Brut* 1986 is a decent wine with fine small bubbles and a round mature taste. The *Cuvée Royale Chardonnay*, made from Cramant, Oger, and Le Mesnil-sur-Oger grapes, is subtle, delicate, and ripe; while the *vintage-dated Cuvée Commodore* is produced by very traditional methods,

De Castellane crenellated tower in Epernay

including the use of a clamped cork rather than a crown cap to stopper the wine during its second fermentation in bottle: the aroma of the 1986 is nutty and honeyed, the flavor expansive and mouth-filling with a note of exotic fruits. The 1982 *Cuvée Florens de Castellane* is a 100 percent Chardonnay champagne at the peak of its maturity.

Brut Croix Rouge de Saint André

	Epernay
	1.5 million bottles
★	good quality

STYLES

NON-VINTAGE

BRUT CROIX ROUGE
DE SAINT ANDRÉ

CUVÉE ROYALE
CHARDONNAY

ROSÉ

ROSÉ CROIX ROUGE DE
SAINT ANDRÉ

VINTAGE

BRUT CROIX ROUGE
DE SAINT ANDRÉ
(1986)

CUVÉE COMMODORE
(1986)

PRESTIGE

CUVÉE FLORENS DE
CASTELLANE (1982)

◄ *Florens de Castellane 1982*

CHARLES DE CAZANOVE

Founded at Avize in 1811 by Charles de Cazanove, this firm has seen a revival since the Lombard family bought it from Moët-Hennessey in 1985.

A lot of money has been invested in modern equipment, and the house style here is for full, fruity champagnes with no hint of austerity. Pinot Noir dominates the *Brut Classique*, a full-bodied wine with lively bubbles and lots of primary red fruit flavor; the *Vintage Brut* 1985 is in the same mold, though as you would expect, the extra age and better-class grapes (mostly Pinot Noir) make it more concentrated and long-flavored. The *Brut Azur* puts the Chardonnay in the driver's seat. It had a surprisingly deep, evolved color on the one occasion I tasted it (January 1994) and the bubbles died quickly, so perhaps it was a dud bottle. The *Brut Rosé*, deep salmon-pink, is vibrantly fruity in the de Cazanove style. The prestige *Stradivarius, Tête de Cuvée, Brut* 1985 (not tasted) is made from 70 percent Chardonnay and 30 percent Pinot Noir.

⊕ Epernay

🍾 1.9 million bottles

★ good quality

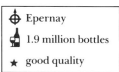

Brut 1985 ▶

STYLES

NON-VINTAGE	VINTAGE
BRUT CLASSIQUE	VINTAGE BRUT (1985)
BRUT AZUR	**PRESTIGE**
ROSÉ	STRADIVARIUS, TÊTE
ROSÉ BRUT	DE CUVÉE, BRUT (1985)

Stradivarius Tête de Cuvée 1985

Brut 1985

Brut Azur   *Rosé Brut*

GUY DE CHASSEY

Guy de Chassey ran this very small firm until his death in June 1993. His daughters Marie-Odile and Monique carry the torch of quality.

The De Chassey sisters produce an excellent full-bodied champagne from their own fruit, buying none in. The predominant Pinot Noir blend is based on 100 percent rated grapes grown in their *grand cru* vineyards at Louvois. The *Grand Cru Brut* is usually the product of a single vintage with some reserve wines occasionally added. They sometimes make wines which they label as vintage. These are generally later disgorged than the so-called "non-vintage" blends.

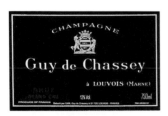

Grand Cru Brut

⊕	Louvois
🍾	40,000 bottles
★★	excellent quality

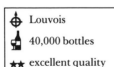

STYLES

NON-VINTAGE
GRAND CRU BRUT

Grand Cru Brut (Louvois monocru) ▶

DE VENOGE

Founded in 1837, de Venoge is housed in very grand premises on Epernay's Avenue de Champagne. By contrast, the wines have a reputation for being decent and workmanlike.

*D*uring the early 1980s, de Venoge became the plaything of the big groups and its stocks were seriously depleted. Since the arrival of Thierry Mantoux, an innovative marketeer, and managing director since 1986, quality has steadily improved. These are now handsomely packaged, easy-to-drink champagnes in an upfront fruity style of real street appeal. While de Venoge only occasionally scales the heights of excellence, there are no bad bottles from this source.

The *Cordon Bleu Brut* is a straightforward champagne, full of primary Pinot Noir fruit, though it is not truly dry (perhaps because of a higher than average *dosage*). The *Blanc de Noirs* (100 percent Pinot Noir) is a flattering, undemanding wine,

Princesse Rosé

Blanc de Noirs Brut

STYLES

NON-VINTAGE	**ROSÉ**
CORDON BLEU BRUT	PRINCESSE ROSÉ
BLANC DE NOIRS	**PRESTIGE**
VINTAGE	CHAMPAGNE DES
VINTAGE BRUT (1986)	PRINCES BLANC DE
BLANC DE BLANCS (1983)	BLANCS (1985)

but a little light considering its composition. The *Vintage Brut 1986* has a full, evolved, mature flavor and some complexity; again it seems quite highly dosed. Easily the best champagnes here are the various *Blancs de Blancs*, especially the vintage-dated 1983 which is mellow and ripe yet vigorously alive. I have not tasted the *Champagne des Princes Blanc de Blancs* 1985 which is highly regarded by the *Guide Hachette* and described as "rich, fresh, lightly smoked, very fruity, as ample as it is long." The *Princesse Rosé* is an innovative wine, the palest shade of pink, made from Chardonnay grapes.

⊕	Epernay
🍾	1.2 million bottles
★	good quality

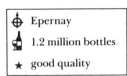

Blanc de Blancs 1983

De Venoge Cordon Bleu

Vintage Brut 1986 ▶

DELAMOTTE

The sixth oldest champagne house, founded in 1760, Delamotte is based in a fine 18th-century property at Le Mesnil-sur-Oger on the Côte des Blancs.

Long associated with Lanson, this little firm with a big reputation among connoisseurs has been owned since 1948 by the de Nonancourt family of Laurent-Perrier. Delamotte has 12 acres of *grand cru* Chardonnay at Le Mesnil. This vineyard produces only about one-fifth of the company's needs, but it firmly acts as a benchmark for nearly all the champagnes in the

⊕ Le Mesnil-sur-Oger

🍾 200,000 bottles

★★ excellent quality

Brut

Delamotte Coat of Arms

range, which are Chardonnay-influenced, fine, fresh and long-lived. In 1989, Laurent-Perrier bought Salon, an even smaller house than Delamotte, but one which produces the greatest of all *Blanc de Blancs*. Delamotte and Salon – immediate neighbors in Le Mesnil – are managed by Bertrand de Fleurian.

The non-vintage *Brut* (half Chardonnay, half black grapes) has very fine bubbles, a touch of apricot on the nose, and a very fresh yet rounded flavor. The *Brut Rosé* is the only wine made from pure Pinot Noir (100 percent); its flavor is redolent of raspberries. The non-vintage *Blanc de Blancs*, pale in color, is very dry, brisk, and racy but with a flattering richness on the after-taste. The *Blanc de Blancs* is a big, powerful wine with a scent of peaches; very deep-flavored and still young-tasting; it should be kept until at least 1995 before pulling the cork. The top-of-the-range *Nicolas Louis Delamotte* is officially a non-vintage wine, although it mostly comes from the 1982 harvest – a textbook example of ripe but still fresh *Blanc de Blancs* which has at least another 10 years of life ahead of it.

STYLES
NON-VINTAGE
BRUT
BLANC DE BLANCS
ROSÉ
BRUT ROSÉ
VINTAGE
BLANC DE BLANCS (1985)
PRESTIGE
NICOLAS LOUIS DELAMOTTE

Brut: half Chardonnay, half black grapes ▶

DELBECK

Frederick Delbeck founded this house in 1832. It still produces a top-flight champagne in a generous, fruity, supple yet complex style.

Frederick Delbeck quickly joined the 19th-century champagne establishment by marrying Balsamie Ponsardin, niece of the great widow Clicquot. In 1838, Delbeck was chosen as the champagne of the Royal Bourbon Court of France: King Louis-Philippe described it as the most exquisite sparkling wine he had ever drunk. The *marque* disappeared from sale for 30 years from the early 1960s. In 1993, the firm was bought by Marquis François d'Aulan who wanted to return to the champagne trade, having sold his interests in Piper-Heidsieck to the Rémy Martin group four years earlier.

Key quality factors in Delbeck champagnes are the house's ownership of 10.6 acres of *grand cru* vineyards in Verzenay on the Montagne de Reims, and reserve stocks of wine representing over six years of annual sales. Continuity of expertise has

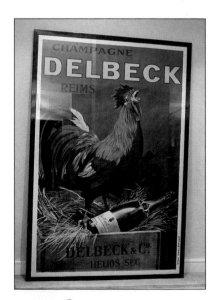

Old Delbeck poster

been assured by retaining the consultant services of Jacques Gauthier, *chef de caves* at Delbeck for 40 years.

Brut Héritage (non-vintage) is composed of 70 percent Pinot Noir and 30 percent Chardonnay with up to 20 percent reserve wines. It is a beautifully blended champagne, strongly fruity but supple, body and finesse in textbook balance, and with a clean durable finish. *Brut Héritage Rosé*, predominantly Pinot Noir, of which 20 percent is traditionally vinified on the grape skins, has a pastel-pink color and speaks refinement. *Brut Vintage* 1985 (65 percent Pinot Noir, 35 percent Chardonnay) is a sleeping giant, a potentially magnificent wine with terrific depth of flavor and life-giving acidity. It should be kept until at least 1995 and will provide superb drinking in 2000.

Delbeck Brut Vintage 1985

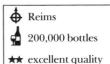

✦ Reims

🍾 200,000 bottles

★★ excellent quality

STYLES

NON-VINTAGE
BRUT HÉRITAGE

ROSÉ
BRUT HÉRITAGE ROSÉ

VINTAGE
BRUT VINTAGE (1985)

Brut Héritage ▶

DEUTZ

*Deutz wines, like the Deutz family, are restrained, subtle,
and understated.*

*L*ike many *grandes marques*, this house was founded by young
entrepreneurs of German origin who moved west to seek
their fortune in Champagne. William Deutz and Pierre
Geldermann, both natives of Aachen, established a champagne
business at Ay in 1838. Deutz, who had previously worked for
Bollinger, brought expertise to the partnership, Geldermann
brought the capital.

The firm's cellars were badly damaged during the Champagne riots of 1911. This scarring experience for his prede-
cessors may have driven André Lallier-Deutz, the current head
of the company, to diversify his wine interests 70 years later
during the boom time of the 1980s. Among his acquisitions at
this time were the Rhône shippers Delas Frères and sparkling-
wine companies in California and New Zealand. But with the

Rosé Brut 1988

Brut 1988

STYLES	
NON-VINTAGE	**PRESTIGE**
BRUT	CUVÉE WILLIAM
KOSHER BRUT	DEUTZ (1985)
VINTAGE	CUVÉE WILLIAM
BRUT (1988)	DEUTZ ROSÉ (1985)
BLANC DE BLANCS	
(1988)	
ROSÉ (1988)	

recession that affected the champagne industry in the wake of the 1991 Persian Gulf War, Deutz's worldwide operations began to look overextended, and in 1993 Louis Roederer bought a 63 percent stake in the company.

Despite its broad international outlook, Deutz is one of the more discreet *grandes marques* and is certainly not a firm which likes to sponsor motor races where the winners shower their rivals with precious champagne. However, in recent tastings, the non-vintage *Brut* has seemed below par, with an aggressive acidity that makes one ask how long this cuvée has aged in the bottle. The vintage wines are another matter. The 1988 *Blanc de Blancs*, made from the best grapes from the *grands crus* of the Côte des Blancs, is a wonderful champagne, light, exquisitely elegant, but with a profundity of flavors which will intensify until the year 2000. The 1988 *Brut* has complex near-Burgundian aromas shaped by 60 percent Pinot Noir in the blend, and is long and persistent on the palate. The 1988 *Rosé* (100 percent Pinot Noir) is very fruity and powerful, a wine for richly flavored shellfish like crab, and, best of all, coulibiac of salmon. The prestige *Cuvée William Deutz*, made only in great years like 1982 and 1985, is an impressive wine for sure but, like many prestige cuvées, is not worth the extra price over, say, the superb *Blanc de Blancs*. An unusual addition to the range is Deutz's non-vintage *Kosher Brut*.

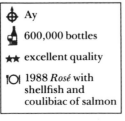

⊕ Ay

🍾 600,000 bottles

★★ excellent quality

🍽 1988 *Rosé* with shellfish and coulibiac of salmon

Brut ▶

DEVAUX

Everything about this immaculate operation inspires confidence, as modern techniques are allied to traditional principles of classic champagne-making.

Veuve Devaux is the flagship brand of the Union Auboise based in unfashionable Bar-sur-Seine, 70 miles southeast of Epernay. This first-rate Aube cooperative is currently producing excellent champagnes which in blind tastings more than hold their own in competition with counterparts from the Marne. The Union is a powerful grouping of 750 member-growers farming 3,212 acres of exclusively Aubois vineyards, planted with 85 percent Pinot Noir, 12 percent Chardonnay, and just 3 percent Pinot Meunier. About one-third of production is exported, mainly to Great Britain, and there is a burgeoning market in the United States, for these wines offer an exceptional value for money.

Crucially, all the Devaux cuvées are properly aged in the bottle before sale. *Grande Réserve Brut*, aged for three years, is a blend of 50 different *crus*; green-gold in color, it is a model standard wine, a restrained note of yeasty complexity in textbook balance with fresh fruit flavors and crisp acidity. *Cuvée*

Grande Réserve Brut

Millésimée, currently the 1988, is atypically a Chardonnay-influenced wine and racier than most from the Aube. *Cuvée Rosé*, pink with orange tints, is full of primary peachy fruit, while the 1985 *Cuvée Spéciale Rosé* is subtly vinous but lively. The top-of-the-range 1985 *Cuvée Spéciale Brut*, a classic blend of Pinot Noir and Chardonnay in equal parts, will go on improving for some years yet. The Union Auboise also vinify the rare and expensive still *Rosé des Riceys*, something of a curiosity. Its bitter-sweet mandarin flavor should not be missed by wine-lovers in search of a new experience, though bottles are hard to find as production is tiny.

 Bar-sur-Seine

 2 million bottles

★★ excellent quality

STYLES

NON-VINTAGE

GRANDE RÉSERVE BRUT

VINTAGE

CUVÉE MILLÉSIMÉE
(currently 1988)

CUVÉE SPÉCIALE ROSÉ
(1985)

ROSÉ DES RICEYS

ROSÉ

CUVÉE ROSÉ

PRESTIGE

CUVÉE SPÉCIALE BRUT
(1985)

Grande Réserve Brut: a well-aged non-vintage ▶

DRAPPIER

---

*Vignerons at Urville since the time of Napoleon, the
Drappiers are now one of the leading grower-merchants
of the Aube.*

*D*rappier champagnes are highly distinctive and hedonistic
with a red fruit flavor that comes from ripe Pinot Noir
grapes grown on the rich Aubois soils. Generosity of flavor
rather than austere finesse is the Drappier style. It certainly
appealed to General de Gaulle, who was a regular customer
while he was living in retirement at nearby Colombey-les-Deux
Eglises. In the 1990s the Drappiers have built important new
markets for their wines in Great Britain and Japan.

The heart of this close-knit family business is the Urville
domaine, housing 12th-century cellars and vineyards which
now extend to 86 acres, mainly planted with Pinot Noir. Young
Michel Drappier, a Dijon-trained oenologist, runs the whole
business with immaculate care and quiet flair. His dark film-
star good looks belie a terrific capacity for hard work, and he is
one of the most open-minded and informative of wine-makers.
The winery is modern and pristine, but the champagnes produced are not just technically correct, they have real personality.

The non-vintage *Carte Blanche* is made from 90 percent

An Aube village well known for Pinot Noir

STYLES

NON-VINTAGE	VINTAGE
CARTE BLANCHE	CARTE D'OR (1988)
SIGNATURE BLANC DE BLANCS	**PRESTIGE**
ROSÉ	GRANDE SENDRÉE (1988; recommended earlier vintages: 1985, 1983)
VAL DES DESMOISELLES ROSÉ	

⊕ Urville

🍾 600,000 bottles

★★ excellent quality

Grande Sendrée 1982: a great year

Grande Sendrée 1988

Carte d'Or Brut: rich, full-flavored Pinot Noir champagne ▶

Pinot Noir and 10 percent Pinot Meunier, the latter giving a spicy note to this rounded, supple champagne. The 1988 *Carte d'Or*, like all Drappier vintage wines, carries the date of *dégorgement* on the label. Tasted in January 1994, ten months after being disgorged, the 1988 showed a lot of promise with that typical red fruit flavor balanced with excellent acidity. The *Signature Blanc de Blancs*, by contrast, seems to me to be the least interesting of the wines from the Drappiers, who are, after all, Pinot Noir specialists. No doubts, though, about the *Grande Sendrée* prestige cuvée, which in years like 1983 and 1985 is a magnificent, sensuous mouthful, still predominantly Pinot Noir but also with a good amount of Chardonnay (45 percent). The recently released *Grande Sendrée* 1988 needs to be kept until 1996 before pulling the cork. The pink *Val des Desmoiselles* is one of the few rosé champagnes still made by the *saignée* method, in which the wine is tinted pink by putting the black Pinot Noir grape skins in contact with the juice for a couple of days prior to fermentation. Rose-petal pink in color, this lovely wine is yet another celebration of the seductive charms of Aubois Pinot Noir.

Carte D'Or

◀ *Grande Sendrée 1988: keenly priced prestige cuvée*

DANIEL DUMONT

*Daniel Dumont is one of the most interesting producers
on the Montagne de Reims, for, as a nurseryman,
working with his two sons, Daniel
raises over 200,000 vines every year
for sale to other producers.*

His knowledge of the clones and varieties
of vines allows Daniel Dumont to select
the best for his own wine production. As a
result, his grapes are extremely healthy and his
champagnes exceptionally pure-flavored.

It shows in the glass. At a tasting at Les
Saveurs restaurant in London in January 1994,
his *Cuvée d'Excellence* 1986 was the star of a line-
up that included several *grandes marques*. Made
from a classic blend of *premier cru* grapes
(Chardonnay predominating), this wine had
everything: silky texture, mouth-filling
richness, superb balancing acidity; no trace

STYLES
NON-VINTAGE
DEMI-SEC
GRANDE RÉSERVE
ROSÉ
GRANDE RÉSERVE ROSÉ
VINTAGE
BRUT RÉSERVE (1988)
PRESTIGE
CUVÉE D'EXCELLENCE (1986)

*Cuvée d'Excellence 1986 –
exceptional cuvée* ▶

Brut Réserve 1988

Grande Réserve

Cuvée d'Excellence 1986

Grande Réserve Rosé

of bitterness. The *Cuvée de Réserve* 1988 is a more forward wine of primary fruit flavors, a proportion of the grapes coming from the smaller holdings in the Côteaux des Sézannais and the Vallée de la Marne. The *Grande Réserve Rosé* is one of the few pink champagnes still made by the traditional method: the grape skins remain in contact with the juice for 24 hours or so, to tint the wine naturally to the desired color. It is a great food wine, its exuberant red fruit flavors of Pinot Noir and Pinot Meunier giving it enough character to match dishes as different as Szechwan pork, blanquette de veau, or salmon in any guise. Daniel also makes a honey-and-almond-flavored *Demi-Sec* that is a more exciting partner for Christmas cake than a cup of tea.

⊕ Rilly-la-Montagne

🍾 50,000 bottles

★★ excellent quality

🍽 *Grande Réserve Rosé* with Szechwan pork

NICOLAS
FEUILLATTE

*This brand was created in the early 1970s by Nicolas Feuillatte,
a globe-trotting entrepreneur who has always seemed
as much at home in the penthouses of Manhattan
as on the vineyard slopes of Champagne.*

At the age of 21, Feuillatte moved to New York where he made his fortune, originally in the coffee trade. In 1970 he sold out and took a year's sabbatical in Sydney. Shortly afterwards he inherited a 30-acre vineyard in Bouleuse which, with an eye for self-promotion, he called Domaine St. Nicolas.

Feuillatte became a major player in the champagne trade in 1976 when he joined forces with the Centre Vinicole de la Champagne. The C.V.C, based at Chouilly in the Côte des Blancs, is a vast cooperative-conglomerate whose 4,000 member-growers bring the juice of their 3,953 acres of vineyards to the company for vinification. These vignerons claim to make about 5 percent of the total production of champagne. What is certain is that in terms of the quality and variety of the *crus* available to him, Feuillatte has excellent grapes to call on, from the Montagne de Reims, the Côte des Blancs, and the Vallée de la Marne.

⊕ Chouilly

🍾 13 million bottles

★ good quality

Brut Premier Cru ▶

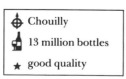

Brut Premier Cru 1982   *Brut Rosé Premier Cru*

Feuillatte's philosophy of champagne is that "it is a natural part of life." Initially sceptical both of this "Madison Avenue" phrase and of the claims of the brand to the making of wines of high quality – the C.V.C now produces 13 million bottles of champagne annually – I was subsequently impressed by the best of the Feuillatte range at a tasting at Les Saveurs Restaurant, London, in December 1993.

These champagnes have an immediacy of appeal which combines a lively *mousse*, direct fruit, and clean acidity. The *Brut Premier Cru* is an excellent and flattering non-vintage wine: the bubbles, foaming to the eye and creamy to the palate, are a delight; there is a distinctive whiff of orange and mandarin; and the taste is rich but invigorating. The non-vintage *Blanc de Blancs* seems to need much more bottle age, having the raw edge of young Chardonnay, and the *Rosé* is frankly disappointing with its orange tint and rather cosmetic flavor. The 1983 *Cuvée Spéciale Palmes d'Or* shows the complexity of its classic blend (40 percent Pinot Noir, 40 percent Chardonnay, 20 percent Pinot Meunier) allied to a clear definition of fruit flavors and the glorious vinosity of a fully mature champagne from a great year. This superb wine (worth three stars) is better and cheaper than the top-of-the-range *Cuvée Prestige*.

STYLES

NON-VINTAGE	PRESTIGE
BRUT PREMIER CRU	**CUVÉE PALMES D'OR**
CHARDONNAY BLANC DE BLANCS	**PREMIER CRU (1983, 1985)**
ROSÉ	**CUVÉE PRESTIGE (1983, 1982)**
BRUT PREMIER CRU ROSÉ (NV)	

GEORGE GARDET

---

*A small family business established in 1890 and now
based in a modern winery at Chigny-les-Roses, George
Gardet buys in mainly 100-percent rated grapes
from the Montagne de Reims.*

The Gardet family employs very traditional wine-making methods, with all the champagnes marked with the year of disgorging. The wines are aged for a very long time in the bottle. The vintage champagnes are of an exceptional quality, showing complex, tertiary, almost "animal" aromas and flavors. The 1983 has an impressive vinosity which always shows well in blind tastings. The *Rosé Brut* (100 percent Pinot Noir) is made by skin contact. Personally, I find it has almost too much flavor for its own good, *mais à chacun son goût*. Gardet champagnes are also sold under a second name, Boucheron. The quality is just as good.

⊕ Chigny-les-Roses

🍾 600,000 bottles

★★ excellent quality

STYLES

NON-VINTAGE
BRUT SPÉCIAL

ROSÉ
ROSÉ BRUT (NV)

VINTAGE
VINTAGE (1983)

Vintage 1983 ▶

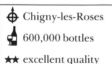

GATINOIS

Champagne production in Ay, famous for its grand
cru *Pinot Noir grapes, is dominated by great houses like
Bollinger, and there are now only 12 small growers in the
commune making and marketing their own champagnes.*

One of the best small growers in Ay is Pierre Cheval-Gatinois,
who looks more like a technocrat than a *vigneron*. Pierre
was born in the vineless neighboring Ardennes but came to
Champagne as a young man, fell in love with Ay, and married
a local girl whose family had been champagne growers here
since 1696.

He now farms his 17-acre vineyard, all classed as *grand cru*,
of which 90 percent is Pinot Noir grown on the uplands, but
with 10 percent Chardonnay planted on more chalky soil at the
bottom of the slopes. His champagnes are deeply colored and
generously flavored, their essential red fruit taste being that of
great Pinot Noir made in tiny quantities from old vines. In
exceptional years like 1989 and 1990 he makes an excellent still
red wine (100 percent Pinot Noir) which is fermented and
aged in newish small oak barrels.

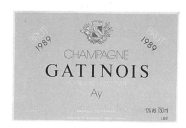

Gatinois Millésimée 1989

The non-vintage *Gatinois Grand Cru, Ay, Tradition Brut*, though officially a white champagne, has a perceptible pinkish tinge and an assertive yet round fruitiness which is the result of the intricate blending of wines from 29 *lieu-dits* (named vineyard sites) in the Gatinois vineyards and three years' aging before release. A big wine for food, especially slow-cooked poultry with a cream sauce is *Gatinois Réserve*, a blend of the 1987 and 1988 vintages. It is more vinous owing to longer aging in the bottle, while *Gatinois Millésimé* 1988 (a classic vintage) is fine and delicate.

 Ay

30,000 bottles

★★ excellent quality

|O| *Gatinois Réserve* with poulard à la crème

STYLES

NON-VINTAGE

GATINOIS GRAND CRU, TRADITION BRUT

VINTAGE

GATINOIS GRAND CRU, RÉSERVE

GATINOIS MILLÉSIMÉ (1988)

GATINOIS COTEAUX CHAMPENOIS (1989, 1990)

Grand Cru Tradition Brut: Ay monocru ▶

GOSSET

*The Gossets have been making wine in Ay since 1584, so
it is not surprising that theirs are traditional
champagnes, lush, rich, and old-fashioned.*

The firm owns 30 acres of choice vineyards on the Montagne
de Reims, but buys in most of its grapes from 30 different
crus, especially Chardonnays from the Côte des Blancs. After
four centuries of family ownership, control of the firm passed
to Max Cointreau of Frapin Cognac in 1994.

Gosset wines are built to last (the malolactic fermentation is
avoided to ensure longevity) and are aged for an exceptionally

⊕	Ay
🍾	500,000 bottles
★★	excellent quality
🍽	*Grande Réserve* with roast pheasant or partridge

Brut Réserve

STYLES	
NON-VINTAGE	**ROSÉ**
BRUT RÉSERVE	GRAND ROSÉ (NV)
GRANDE RÉSERVE	**VINTAGE**
	GRAND MILLÉSIMÉ (1983)

long time in the bottle. The British critic Jane MacQuitty is right to warn that their musky style is not for everyone. Personally speaking, I feel that the standard *Brut Réserve* wins more marks for flavor than for elegance, and the much-vaunted 1983 *Grand Millésimé* does have a muskiness that leaves me cold. However, there is one great wine from Gosset, the *Grande Réserve*, which has slightly more Pinot Noir than Chardonnay and is a blend of the 1984, 1985, and 1986 vintages. Its rich multi-layered flavors are striking proof that a non-vintage champagne can be better than one from a single year. Terrific with a dish like roast pheasant or partridge.

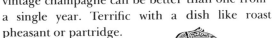

1985 Brut

Brut Rosé

Brut Rosé ▶

George Goulet

Famous as the provider of the late King George VI's favorite bubbly, George Goulet is a rare and happy instance of a champagne house that has regained its independence after years of control by the Besserat de Bellefon group.

he house is now owned by a family of growers around Verzenay on the Montagne de Reims. Their champagne is highly prized among connoisseurs, in Great Britain especially. Goulet's non-vintage *Extra Quality Brut*, though made from 80 percent Pinot Noir of *grand* and *premier cru* ratings, tasted heavy, ponderous, and lifeless at a tasting at Les Saveurs Restaurant in December 1993. The vintage champagnes, white and pink, are very much better – big burly wines with very long flavors – and especially successful in the 1985 vintage.

 Verzenay

100,000 bottles

★ good quality

STYLES

NON-VINTAGE
EXTRA QUALITY BRUT

ROSÉ
EXTRA QUALITY BRUT
ROSÉ (1985)

VINTAGE
EXTRA QUALITY BRUT
(1985)

Extra Quality Brut ▶

ALFRED GRATIEN

Alfred Gratien is a highly individual company. Walking along the bare boards of the firm's shabby offices today, one sees that very little has changed since Alfred Gratien, a native of Saumur, opened his champagne business on Epernay's rue Maurice Cerveaux in 1867.

*D*on't be disconcerted. This modest home provides a range of truly excellent champagnes made with the conviction that the old ways are best.

The key job of *chef de caves* has been in the same family for five generations. The present incumbent, Jean-Pierre Jaeger, insists that his champagnes are totally fermented in wood, and they are then given plenty of aging in the bottle before release.

The non-vintage *Alfred Gratien Brut* has a light straw-yellow color and a spicy, fresh-bread bouquet which almost certainly comes from the very high percentage of Pinot Meunier in the blend, though Jean-Pierre is cagey about revealing the exact amount. Freshness and finesse is given by adding about 30

STYLES	
NON-VINTAGE	**PRESTIGE**
ALFRED GRATIEN BRUT	ALFRED GRATIEN CUVÉE PARADIS
VINTAGE	
ALFRED GRATIEN BRUT (1983)	

Alfred Gratien Brut

percent Chardonnay, allied to the practice at Gratien of avoiding the malolactic fermentation to ensure optimum vitality in all the wines.

For the vintage wines at Gratien at least 50 percent Chardonnay is used in the blend, and the house style of these is elegant, racy, and very long-lived. The prestige *Alfred Gratien Cuvée Paradis* is a masterpiece which deserves the highest star rating. Although this wine does not carry a vintage label, the base is the 1985 vintage. The color is a lovely sustained lemon-gold, the *mousse* ultra delicate, the flavor extremely refined, long, and persistent: all this has a lot to do with the contribution of Chardonnay (71 percent) to the blend.

The 1983 *Alfred Gratien Brut* has a more evolved straw-yellow color and a riper, fuller flavor (about one-third of the blend is Pinot Noir), but this near-mature wine, which will reach its best in 1994 or 1995, still has the signature vintage Gratien taste of top-notch Chardonnay-based champagne.

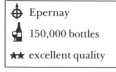

⊕ Epernay

🍾 150,000 bottles

★★ excellent quality

◄ *Alfred Gratien Brut*

EMILE HAMM

Founded in 1910 by an Ay grower whose father came from Alsace, the firm achieved négociant status in 1930 and is now run by the fourth generation of the family.

Emile Hamm owns 8.6 acres of highly rated Ay vineyards but buys in most of its grapes. Nearly all the champagnes are genuinely very dry with a *dosage* of less than 1 percent. The non-vintage *Sélection Brut* is made from a blend of minor *crus*, with about one-third of Chardonnay grapes from the second pressings. The *Premier Cru Réserve* is recommended; a 60:40 blend of Pinot Noir and Chardonnay, it has a pleasantly yeasty nose and youthful fruit flavors. The 1987, of similar composition, is a decent effort in a difficult year: the high acidity typical of the vintage is easing to reveal a well-balanced, gently evolved flavor.

⊕ Ay

240,000 bottles

★ good quality

STYLES

NON-VINTAGE
SÉLECTION BRUT
PREMIER CRU
RÉSERVE BRUT
ROSÉ
ROSÉ BRUT
VINTAGE
VINTAGE (1987)

Premier Cru Réserve Brut ▶

CHARLES
HEIDSIECK

This prestigious grande marque *house is justly famed
on both sides of the Atlantic for its rich, hedonistic, full-
flavored champagnes that make excellent partners to
fine cusine.*

harles-Camille Heidsieck was one of the great champagne
salesmen. With his brother-in-law Ernest Henriot, he
founded this house in 1851 and looked across the Atlantic for
new customers. The following year he made the first of four
journeys to the United States. By the start of the Civil War he
was selling 300,000 bottles of champagne a year from New
York to Louisiana. But it all ended in tears in 1861 when he was
arrested by the Unionists in New Orleans while in possession
of letters from French manufacturers offering to supply cloth-
ing to the Confederate armies. After four months in a swampy
Mississippi jail, Charles-Camille returned to France a near-
ruined man. But the firm did survive. Charles-Camille's sons
and grandsons found new markets in Europe, the Far East and
South America, while developing sales in the United States.

The family ran the firm until 1976 when Joseph Henriot,
descendant of Ernest, took control. In 1985 Charles Heidsieck

Brut Réserve

Vintage Brut 1985

Blanc des Millénaires 1983

was sold to the Rémy-Martin group, which already owned Krug. Under the new ownership the quality of the wines has improved enormously; the firm's non-vintage champagne is much richer than it used to be and is one of the very best on the market. The main reason for the improvement is that Rémy's financial strength has allowed Daniel Thibault, Charles Heidsieck's *chef de caves*, to buy the best grapes, and, crucially, to increase his stocks of reserve wines. Thibault has been lionized by the press as a blender of exceptional talent, even as a magician. But as he says, "*chefs de caves* are not sorcerers, it's the raw material, the grapes, which make the quality of champagne."

Before the Rémy takeover, Charles Heidsieck owned no vineyards, but it has since acquired nearly 74 acres of prime sites in Oger, on the Côte des Blancs, and Ambonnay and Bouzy on the Montagne. This has given the company a good start toward their goal of greater direct control over the quality of the harvest.

The outstanding quality of the non-vintage *Charles Heidsieck Brut Réserve* is the result of careful natural vinification and the complexity of the blend. The wines are made entirely from the first pressings of the grapes, the use of the second pressings having been entirely eliminated since 1985. Alcoholic fermentation takes place in stainless steel, after which technical treatments of the wines are kept to a minimum to preserve their natural character.

The *Brut Réserve* blend is composed of up to 300 different components, of which 40 percent are reserve wines

Blanc des Millénaires Blanc de Blancs 1983: one of the best Chardonnay champagnes on the market ▶

from older vintages. These wines shape the unmistakable vanilla-and-honey flavor of the finished champagne – very much the Charles Heidsieck style – and achieved without the use of wood. The grape mix is three-quarters Pinot Noir and Pinot Meunier and a quarter Chardonnay, the latter maintaining the champagne's zip while adding a whiff of filberts. Critics complain that the *Brut Réserve* is overpriced, which seems wide of the mark for a champagne of remarkable quality costing less than inferior vintage wines from other houses.

The point is reinforced when tasting the *Charles Heidsieck Vintage* 1985, a less complex wine than the *Brut Réserve*. Perversely, the *Rosé Vintage* 1985 is exceptional; of pale onion-skin color and subtle and refined rather than vibrantly fruity, it is one pink champagne which really improves with age and should provide excellent drinking in 1995–96. The 1983 *Blanc des Millénaires* (100 percent Chardonnay) is one of the best *Blanc de Blancs* around – a typical Thibault creation, wonderfully rich and creamy with flavors of exotic fruits to win over drinkers who find pure Chardonnay champagnes austere. Hard to find outside a wine auction room but a collector's dream is the 1981 *Charles Heidsieck Cuvée la Royale*, essentially the taste of great old Pinot Noir dominated champagne with an unforgettable smell of roasted coffee beans. That may not sound inviting, so all that I can say is that I would travel the 300 miles from London to Reims just to taste it again.

⊕ Reims

🍾 3 million bottles

★★ the best quality available

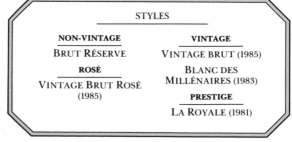

STYLES

NON-VINTAGE	VINTAGE
BRUT RÉSERVE	VINTAGE BRUT (1985)
ROSÉ	BLANC DES MILLÉNAIRES (1983)
VINTAGE BRUT ROSÉ (1985)	PRESTIGE
	LA ROYALE (1981)

HEIDSIECK MONOPOLE

Founded by Henri-Louis Walbaum in 1834, this firm was originally known as Heidsieck & Co. The "Monopole" tag was added in 1923 by a new owner, Edouard Mignon of Comptoirs Français.

This company, which has been part of the Seagram group since 1972, shares wine-making facilities with Mumm, a giant of the industry. Yet Heidsieck Monopole still officially has extensive vineyards of its own, some 275 acres, including some prime sites of Pinot Noir in the *grands crus* of Ambonnay, Bouzy, Verzenay, and Verzy on the Montagne de Reims. Although

 Reims

 1.5 million bottles

★ good quality

STYLES

NON-VINTAGE
DRY MONOPOLE BRUT
VINTAGE
DRY MONOPOLE (1987)
DRY MONOPOLE ROSÉ (1988)
PRESTIGE
DIAMANT BLEU (1985, 1982; older recommended vintage 1976)

Dry Monopole Brut ▶

these only account for about one-third of the firm's needs, they provide good base wines for the cuvées and they shape the full rich champagne house style.

The *Dry Monopole Brut* is made from a mix of all three champagne grapes in roughly equal parts, and though there is some disagreement among critics about its consistency, I have always found it discreetly aromatic, round in flavor, and well balanced. The prestige cuvée Diamant Bleu is an immaculately blended wine (50 percent Pinot Noir, 50 percent Chardonnay) the 1976 being particularly impressive. This wine is now something of a collector's item.

Dry Monopole

Dry Monopole 1987

Dry Monopole Rosé 1988

◀ *Diamant Bleu 1982 Prestige Cuvée*

PIPER-HEIDSIECK

Piper-Heidsieck has always been a famous grande
marque *with a big United States following. Now there
are signs that its light, straightforward champagnes are
changing in style, showing richer, more complex tones.*

*I*t is difficult to know quite what to make of Piper-
Heidsieck. Founded in 1834 by Christian Heidsieck, nephew
of Florenz-Ludwig (the paterfamilias of the Heidsieck dynasty),
the firm remained independent until 1989. Yet Piper has rarely
won press plaudits for its champagnes. Most critics see them as
being light and rather austere (until recently they never went
through malolactic fermentation) and lacking richness or
complexity.

But with the takeover of the firm by the Rémy-Cointreau
group in 1989, things have taken a turn for the better. Daniel
Thibault, *chef de caves* at Charles Heidsieck, now makes the
champagnes at Piper, too. They are beginning to become richer
and more generous in flavor, though as a deliberate act of

Brut

Brut Sauvage 1982

STYLES	
NON-VINTAGE	**VINTAGE**
BRUT	BRUT SAUVAGE
	(1982, 1985)
ROSÉ	
ROSÉ BRUT	**PRESTIGE**
	CHAMPAGNE RARE
	(1985)

policy they remain fairly straightforward champagnes of primary fruit with a good flick of acidity.

Easily the best wines here are the vintage cuvées such as the bone-dry *Brut Sauvage* 1982, which although undosed is very naturally flavored and not too austere thanks to the ripeness of the grapes in the blend. The prestige cuvée *Champagne Rare* 1985 is a splendid wine; Chardonnay-dominated, citrussy, racy, and long on the palate, it will develop greatly in bottle until 1996–97. The Thibault-made non-vintage *Rosé Brut* gets very high marks from the 1994 *Guide Hachette*, in which the tasters raved about its aromas of vanilla and tastes of woodland fruit, which suggests lots of reserve wines in the blend.

 Reims

5 million bottles

★ good quality

Prestige Champagne Rare 1985

◀ *Brut Sauvage 1985: bone-dry vintage champagne Chardonnay grapes*

HENRIOT

Henriot champagnes are Chardonnay-influenced, briskly invigorating, definitely dry, and extremely elegant.

Vignerons in the Champagne region since the 17th century and merchants since 1808, the Henriots farm 272 acres of superb vineyards, mainly on the Côte des Blancs but with fine sites on the Montagne de Reims and in the Vallée de la Marne. Joseph Henriot, the present head of the company, is one of the most influential men in the champagne industry, a complex character who is both a passionate guardian of quality and a wheeler-dealer of extreme agility. In 1985 he merged the family Henriot business with that of Veuve Clicquot and directed the two companies, each with separate identities, until 1994. What will he do next?

The one wine that seems out of place in his impressive range is the non-vintage *Souverain Brut*, which is a rather rough-and-ready champagne compared with its classy stable

Non-vintage Blanc de Blancs

1988 Brut

1985 Rosé

Souverain Brut

mates. The non-vintage *Blanc de Blancs* is light and citrussy, ideal as an aperitif. The 1985 *Rosé* is very subtle stuff, made entirely from Chardonnay with 15 percent Bouzy Rouge added. The vintage 1985 *Brut* is a big wine that will improve with age. Henriot uses no Meunier in the blend.

⊕ Reims

🍾 1 million bottles

★★ excellent quality

STYLES

NON-VINTAGE

SOUVERAIN BRUT

BLANC DE BLANCS

VINTAGE

VINTAGE BRUT
(1985, 1988)

ROSÉ (1985)

PRESTIGE

CUVÉE BACCARAT
(1983)

◀ *Non-vintage Blanc de Blancs: an ideal aperitif*

IRROY

This little champagne house, established in 1820, is one of the least known, being completely overshadowed by its parent company, Taittinger.

rroy's lack of fame is good news for the discerning consumer, for these champagnes are decent, well made (largely from Chardonnay grapes) and often a bargain. The *Brut Carte d'Or* is a light and elegant wine for easy drinking, but the star buy is the *Rosé*. With its pale salmon color, its wafting aroma of red fruit, and subtle poised flavor, it quite outshone the pink competition from some much grander houses at a London tasting in December 1993. More's the pity that Irroy recently lost its *grande marque* status.

⊕ Reims

🍾 500,000 bottles

★ good quality

STYLES
NON-VINTAGE
CARTE D'OR BRUT
ROSÉ
NON-VINTAGE ROSÉ

Brut Rosé: excellent Chardonnay-dominated Rosé ▶

JACQUART

One of the major players in the modern champagne industry, Jacquart is a large cooperative-turned-merchant house.

Jacquart is now the sixth biggest champagne producer. Its strength comes from 2,471 acres of vines owned by its 700 member growers, impeccable wine-making, and modern aggressive marketing of the Jacquart label, especially in France. Jacquart produces clean, well-balanced *Brut Tradition*; non-vintage, classy Chardonnay-driven *Brut Sélection*; immaculate *1987 Brut* (a real success in a difficult year); and the prestige *1985 Cuvée Nominée Blanc de Blancs*, a champagne of rare refinement.

 Reims

 10 million bottles

★★ excellent quality

STYLES

NON-VINTAGE

BRUT TRADITION

ROSÉ BRUT

BRUT SÉLECTION

VINTAGE

BRUT 1987

PRESTIGE

CUVÉE NOMINÉ

BLANC DE BLANCS 1985

Brut 1987 ▶

ANDRÉ JACQUART

A leading grower in Le Mesnil, André Jacquart exports his excellent, sharply priced champagnes to the United States, Great Britain, and Japan.

His is essentially a Chardonnay house, the family owning 27 acres in choice vineyards along the Côte des Blancs (including a prime plot in Le Mesnil) with smaller holdings (17 acres) of Pinot Noir and Pinot Meunier in the Vallée de la Marne and the Aube.

The *Carte Blanche Brut* (non-vintage) is the firm's best-known brand, its incisive, dry flavor of top-flight Chardonnay rounded out with the richer tastes of early-maturing Pinot Noir. This impeccably balanced champagne is one of the best buys available. The *Grand Cru Le Mesnil* is the wine of a single year. The 1986 was a model, mature *Blanc de Blancs* for drinking in 1994–95.

⊕ Le Mesnil-sur-Oger

🍾 100,000 bottles

★★ excellent quality

STYLES

NON-VINTAGE

A JACQUART, CARTE BLANCHE BRUT

PRESTIGE

A JACQUART, GRAND CRU LE MESNIL

Carte Blanche N.V. ▶

KRUG

The most prestigious name in champagne. Krug wines have always been deep-flavored, uncompromising, and extremely expensive. Made by the fifth and sixth generations of the family, they need long aging but can taste magnificent when they are 10, 15, even 20 years old.

The house was founded in 1843 by Johann Joseph Krug, a German immigrant from Mainz, who had learned the art of blending at Jacquesson.

The distinctive taste of Krug champagnes – full, rich, and nutty – comes from the highly traditional way in which they are vinified. Krug is the only house which ferments *all* its wines in small oak *barriques*. This process undoubtedly shapes the vinous house style, which is quite unlike any other. But the crucial quality factor here is the family's extremely rigorous approach to the art of blending. The *Krug Grande Cuvée*, the flagship brand of the house, is (as wine-maker Henri Krug puts it), "a blend of the broadest possible dimensions, intricately balancing as many as 40 to 50 different wines from 20 to 25 different growths and six to ten different vintages."

A typical grape mix for *Grande Cuvée* might be 45–55 percent Pinot Noir, 25–35 percent Chardonnay and 15–20 percent Pinot Meunier. The Krugs are great champions of the Pinot Meunier (bought from the cooperative in Leuvrigny) as

Grande Cuvée Presentation Box

they believe it adds fruitiness and spice to the blend. The current *Grande Cuvée* (last tasted January 1994) has returned to top form after one or two disappointments in recent years. The color is a beautiful bright gold, there are scents of toasty vanilla and hazelnut, and the taste seems fresher and more sprightly than it used to be, but with a burgeoning richness.

This brings me to the thorny point of when to drink the wine: for although *Grande Cuvée* is never released until it has at least six years' bottle age, it really does repay keeping for a further year or two before pulling the cork.

The vintage wines are supreme examples of the champagne blender's art – *Grande Cuvée* writ large – and may be recommended without exception because the Krugs are careful to make them only in exceptional years. The currently available 1982 is a powerful wine of intense ripe concentration for drinking in 1995–2000. Of earlier vintages 1979, 1976, 1975, 1973, 1971, and 1969 were especially splendid. For lovers of an "old" wine now in its prime, *Krug Collection* 1964 in magnums is available

STYLES

NON-VINTAGE

KRUG GRANDE CUVÉE

VINTAGE

KRUG VINTAGE (1982)

ROSÉ

KRUG ROSÉ

PRESTIGE

KRUG CLOS DU MESNIL
(1982)

*Krug Clos du Mesnil 1982:
outstanding Blanc de Blancs* ▶

Henri Krug

Krug 1982 vintage

Krug Close du Mesnil 1983

Krug Grande Cuvée

tiny quantities. A certificate signed by Henri Krug is issued to collectors on request.

The *Krug Clos du Mesnil Blanc de Blancs* is produced solely from *grand cru* Chardonnay grapes in a walled vineyard ("clos") at Le Mesnil-sur-Oger, the greatest white wine village of the Côte des Blancs. With financial help from the Rémy-Cointreau group, who now have a controlling interest in Krug, this plum 4.9-acre site was bought by the company in the early 1970s, the first vintage being in 1979. Like all Chardonnay champagnes from Le Mesnil, the Krugs' *Clos* is mouth-puckering and acidic when young, but given 12 to 15 years in bottle it takes on the complexity of a great Corton Charlemagne with bubbles. The 1982 *will* be a very great wine, but do not broach it before the turn of the century.

Krug Rosé, first introduced in 1983, is cast in the same serious mold as the rest of the range. Firmly structured, very fruity and extremely dry, it is intended to accompany fine cuisine. The famous Paris chef Alain Senderens once created an entire meal – from leek-wrapped lobster to a mosaic of veal – around this wine. The Krug 1985 vintage was released in May 1994. It is a stunning wine, fresher and racier than the 1992.

Reims

500,000 bottles

the best quality available

Krug silver dosage measurers and corks

L A N S O N

One of the oldest houses in Champagne, Lanson has always been acclaimed for its quality wines that offered excellent value for money, and outstanding vintage champagnes. But recent changes threaten a downturn.

*L*anson's is a sad story. As recently as 1990 this great house, one of the oldest in Champagne, seemed to have adapted well to the modern world; its best-selling Black Label Brut was a good, reliable wine and its vintage champagnes were some of the best around. But in 1991 Lanson lost all 514 acres of its magnificent vineyards when the firm was sold by the Louis Vuitton-Moët-Hennessy group to a consortium headed by Marne et Champagne. The future style and quality of these champagnes must be in doubt following a recent tasting of the flagship cuvée, the non-vintage *Black Label Brut*, at Les Saveurs Restaurant in January 1994. Speaking personally, I found it a pale shadow of its former self, acidic, immature, and charmless.

Black label Brut

Brut 1985 vintage

Brut Rosé

The *Rosé Brut* seemed cast in the same mold. However, the remaining stocks of the 1985 vintage champagnes should be snapped up quickly, especially the prestige *Noble Cuvée*, which is a magnificent wine and a masterpiece of vigor, richness, and balance made from grapes grown in the family vineyards and vinified without malolactic fermentation to ensure a long life. As a salute to the old days, the firm *just* earns a one-star rating, but urgent action is needed to improve the non-vintage wines if Lanson is to regain its reputation as one of the true *grandes marques*.

Noble Cuvée

	Reims
	5 million bottles
★	good quality

STYLES

NON-VINTAGE
BLACK LABEL BRUT

ROSÉ
ROSÉ

VINTAGE
VINTAGE (1985)

PRESTIGE
NOBLE CUVÉE (1985)

Brut 1985 Vintage ▶

LARMANDIER-
BERNIER

Pierre Larmandier makes some of the most stylish champagnes in the Côte des Blancs, as he has excellent grapes to draw on from the family's 30-acre domaine *spanning the Chardonnay grands crus of Cramant, Chouilly, and Oger.*

*I*n Vertus he grows both Chardonnay and a little Pinot Noir. The average age of the vines is 30 years, though he has a significant number of old vines too. Vinification takes place in stainless steel vats that are temperature-controlled, and all the wines go through malolactic fermentation. They are aged for at least three years in the bottle and are given a low *dosage* at the time of *dégorgement*, after which there is always a resting period of at least three months before shipment. The resulting champagne style is firm and incisive but with a lovely expression of pure-flavored, unadulterated Chardonnay fruit.

The cuvées to earmark from this range are the *Brut Blanc de Blancs Premier Cru*, light, fresh, aromatic (a superb aperitif)

Cramant Grand Cru

Brut Rosé

Brut Premier Cru Blanc de Blancs

and the *Cramant Grand Cru*, more complex and very long on the palate. Larmandier-Bernier champagnes are wines of real class and, being little known outside France and Belgium, are shrewd buys with an excellent quality-to-price ratio. If you are ever in Paris, try them at the Restaurant Benoît in the rue St. Martin (4ème).

Brut Tradition

Blanc de Blancs Premier Cru

 Vertus

85,000 bottles

★★ excellent quality

STYLES
PRESTIGE
BRUT BLANC DE BLANCS PREMIER CRU
CRAMANT GRAND CRU

Brut Blanc de Blancs Premier Cru: incisive Chardonnay Champagne ▶

LAURENT-PERRIER

Like several great champagne houses, Laurent-Perrier owes a lot to resourceful widows. Today, this grande marque *house probably produces the most varied and imaginative range of wines in the whole region. And it has always been a courageous pace-setter.*

*O*n the death of her husband Eugène Laurent in 1887, Mathilde Perrier added her name to his and managed the company successfully for 38 years – in 1914 Veuve Laurent-Perrier was selling 600,000 bottles of excellent champagne a year – but she lost a lot of her family during the First World War and died without children in 1925. Another widow, Marie-Louise de Nonancourt, sister of Victor and Henri Lanson, took over the moribund firm in 1938, intending to hand it over to her son Maurice.

Called to work for the Germans during the occupation of France, Maurice de Nonancourt tried to reach England through Spain but was arrested at the Spanish border and died in the German deportation camp of Oranienburg. His younger brother Bernard spent much of the war in a Maquis Résistance cell in the French Alps, where he learned that to survive in life you have to surround yourself with competent people. When

Barrel cellar at Laurent-Perrier

Bernard de Nonancourt took over Laurent-Perrier in 1948, he was extremely careful in his choice of colleagues to help rebuild the firm. Over the 45 years since then, Laurent-Perrier has grown from a tiny concern into the fourth largest champagne house, with annual sales of about 7 million bottles.

Laurent-Perrier is based in a domaine surrounded by vines at Tours-sur-Marne, 8 miles east of Epernay. The location is significant for, talking to the people who work here, you are left in no doubt that champagne-making is an art but one that depends on great grapes. The firm owns 247 acres of vineyards, which provides about 12 percent of its needs, but relies on an extensive network of growers.

In a bold departure from conventional practice, the firm decided to make a non-vintage prestige cuvée named *Grand Siècle* in 1957 because it believed that a better balanced flavor would be achieved by blending wines from three great years. Ever since, *Grand Siècle* has been a consistently magnificent wine; it is occasionally sold with a vintage label in exceptional years. In 1981, Laurent-Perrier released its first *Cuvée Ultra Brut*, a very dry champagne with no *dosage*. Thus were recreated the "sugarless" champagnes that the house had sold in England (where else?) in the 1890s. You do not

⊕ Tours-sur-Marne

🍾 7 million bottles

★★ the best quality available

Rosé Brut ▶

have to be a diabetic to appreciate this wine for, although bone-dry, it is not astringent since it is always made from the grapes of a ripe year, and on a hot summer evening it is wonderfully refreshing.

This firm is also one of the very few to make pink champagne the hard way – by putting the Pinot Noir grape skins into contact with the juice to obtain the required color. As if that were not enough, it is the leading specialist in the still Coteaux Champenois wines of the region, both white and red. Alain Terrier, Laurent-Perrier's cellarmaster, is one of the most gifted wine-makers I have ever met. Slightly severe and professorial on first acquaintance, this Bordeaux-born oenologist gave me some fascinating insights into the art of blending when I tasted the current releases with him at the domaine in January 1994. Looking at my notes, as they say, it was a stimulating experience.

Here is the race card. The current *Ultra Brut* is a shimmering green-gold color, there is a nose of ripe apricots and in the mouth the flavors are mature, with no hint of aggression. A very high proportion of the wines in the blend come from the 1985 vintage. The *Brut L.P.*, the flagship brand, is especially good at the moment, being essentially made from the hot 1989 vintage. Whiffs of brioche and mandarin orange lead on to a round, rich flavor. The vintage 1988 (53 per cent Chardonnay, 47 percent Pinot Noir) has a mushroomy aroma typical of Pinot Noir, which dominates the flavor

◀ *Grand Siècle: Prestige Cuvée made from a blend of three vintages*

at the moment; however, with further aging the Chardonnay tastes will progressively take over.

The current *Grand Siècle* is predominantly 1988 with smaller proportions of 1985 and 1982. With a light majority of Chardonnary it is very fine, delicate, and well-balanced but with a long, generous aftertaste. The *Grand Siècle exceptionellement millésimé* 1985 is a sensational bottle; this time Pinot Noir (58 percent) dominates the blend, for this grape was extremely ripe in the Champagne region that year, and this wine has a glorious, toasted character. *Grand Siècle Alexandra Rosé* 1982 is a brick-colored rosé champagne of rare vinosity.

STYLES	
NON-VINTAGE	**PRESTIGE**
ULTRA BRUT	GRAND SIÈCLE
BRUT LP	
ROSÉ	GRAND SIÈCLE EXCEPTIONELLEMENT MILLÉSIMÉ (1985)
ROSÉ BRUT	
VINTAGE	GRAND SIÈCLE ALEXANDRA BRUT ROSÉ (1982)
VINTAGE (1988)	

Cuvée Ultra Brut

Brut Vintage 1985

Pinot-Franc: a still Pinot Noir wine

Blanc de Blancs de Chardonnay: a still white wine

R & L LEGRAS

René and Lucien Legras established this elite little champagne business in 1972 – their Grand Cru Blanc de Blancs *is the house champagne of many Michelin-starred restaurants in France. And very good it is too.*

The Legras family, vignerons since the 18th century, own 52 acres of vineyards on the Côte des Blancs. Their Blanc des Blancs has a vital green-gold color, a superfine *mousse*, floral, well defined Chardonnay aromas, a rounded, toasty flavor, and a persistent finish. The prestige *Cuvée St. Vincent* is a rich, evolved Chardonnay champagne with distinctive walnut aromas not unlike Salon. The *Brut Intégral* was one of the first sugarless champagnes released in the 1970s. The current release is flower-scented yet bone dry without being too austere.

⊕ Chouilly

🍾 250,000 bottles

★★ excellent quality

STYLES

NON-VINTAGE
BLANC DE BLANCS
BRUT INTÈGRAL

VINTAGE
VINTAGE-DATED
BLANC DE BLANCS

PRESTIGE
CUVÉE ST.VINCENT

Brut Blanc de Blancs Grand Cru ▶

ABEL LEPITRE

Founded in 1924 by Abel Lepitre and greatly expanded by his son Jacques after the Second World War, this firm had a very good repution in the 1960s, especially for its excellent prestige cuvée Prince A. de Bourbon Parme.

Since 1970, Abel Lepitre has had several owners but it is now part of the Marie Brizard group which also owns the excellent Mareuil-sur-Ay house of Philipponnat. There seems to be a reforming hand at work, for the Lepitre champagnes are once again worth seeking out.

The standard *Brut* (60 percent Pinot Noir, 25 percent Chardonnay, 15 percent Pinot Meunier) has a nicely evolved, nutty nose and its pure fruit flavors are round and full. The *Vintage Brut* 1986 (a classic 60–40 blend of Pinot Noir and Chardonnay) is a very proper glass of mature champagne, honeyed yet fresh. The non-vintage *Cuvée 134* is in the style of the old *crémant* champagnes that established Lepitre's reputation; made from 100 percent Chardonnay with a gentle *mousse*, it is light, incisive, medium-bodied, and ideal as an aperitif. The *vintage-dated Rosé*, currently the 1986, is an assemblage of 55 percent Pinot Noir, 35 percent Chardonnay, with 15 percent Bouzy rouge: subtle stuff.

⊕	Mareuil-sur-Ay
	400,000 bottles
★	good quality

Non-vintage Brut ▶

STYLES

NON-VINTAGE	ROSÉ
BRUT	VINTAGE ROSÉ (1986)
CUVÉE 134	**VINTAGE**
	VINTAGE BRUT (1986)

Cuvée Millésimée 1985

Brut N.V.

Brut Rosé

Vintage Brut 1986

Cuvée 134

CHAMPAGNE

Abel Lepitre

Demi-Sec

MAILLY

---

*Without exception Mailly champagnes have at least
75 percent Pinot Noir in their composition, so the house
style here is a youthful, black-grape
fruitiness.*

This well-known cooperative on the Montagne de Reims, founded in 1929, has 70 members farming altogether 173 acres of vines all within the commune of Mailly and classed as *grand cru*. You either like or dislike the young Pinot-dominated style of Mailly champagnes. Personally, I think several of the cuvées here could do with much more bottle age. Three recommendations: The *Mailly Grand Cru Brut Réserve* is full of primary Pinot Noir fruit, big-flavored, with a slightly rooty vegetal finish; the *Mailly Grand Cru* 1988 is in a similar style to the *Brut Réserve* but with more intensity of flavor (still very young-tasting, though); and, perversely, the best buy is the *Mailly Coteaux Champenois Rouge*, which is a seriously good red wine with a nicely modulated ruby color, and a fine combination of finesse, flavor, and vinosity on both nose and palate.

Cuvée des Echansons

Grand Cru Brut Réserve ▶

Brut Blanc de Noirs

Grand Cru Brut 1988

Grand Cru Brut Réserve

Grand Cru Rosé Brut

Mailly

600,000 bottles

★ good quality

STYLES

NON-VINTAGE

GRAND CRU BRUT RÉSERVE

COTEAUX CHAMPENOIS ROUGE

ROSÉ

GRAND CRU ROSÉ BRUT

VINTAGE

GRAND CRU VINTAGE (1988)

MERCIER

---

*Eugène Mercier was a great promoter who democratized
the image of champagne. He founded this house in 1858,
specializing in mass-produced wines for the general
public. Mercier wines are very good value.*

*M*ercier always thought big: over a 20-year period he built the world's second largest wine barrel in preparation for the Universal Exhibition held in Paris in 1889; it took a team of 24 oxen three weeks to tow the cask to the capital. Yet the great showman is best remembered for the extraordinary cellars he built at the top of the hill on Epernay's Avenue de Champagne. They extend to 10 miles of wide, cool subterranean galleries which you can visit daily on the firm's miniature electric train.

Mercier's family bought a lot of vineyards in the 1950s in the Marne Valley, mainly planted with Pinot Meunier. In 1970 the firm was bought by Moët & Chandon, and is now part of the L.V.M.H. group.

Although Mercier does not reveal the grape mix of its cuvées, it is reasonable to assume that they are mostly based on Pinot Meunier, which accounts for their rich, spicy taste and their keen price. From a decent range, earmark the aromatic *Rosé Brut* with its nice balance of fruit and acidity, the successful *Demi-Sec*, which is clean-tasting and not cloying, and the *Vintage Brut* 1986 which has a ripe Chardonnay-esque character.

Brut 1986 ▶

```
┌─────────────────────────────────────────┐
│                 STYLES                    │
│                                           │
│   NON-VINTAGE           VINTAGE           │
│     BRUT           VINTAGE BRUT (1986)    │
│   DEMI-SEC              PRESTIGE          │
│     ROSÉ           PRESTIGE CUVÉE         │
│   ROSÉ BRUT          BULLE D'OR           │
└─────────────────────────────────────────┘
```

 Epernay

5.7 million bottles

★ good quality

Brut 1986

Brut N.V.

Demi-Sec

Brut Rosé

MOËT & CHANDON

*Moët & Chandon is the giant of the champagne industry
and getting bigger by the minute. Until 1987, with its
subsidiaries Mercier and Ruinart, it accounted for about
a quarter of the region's champagne sales; now, with
Veuve Clicquot and Pommery within the fold, the Moët
group (L.V.M.H.) dominates the export business.*

For such a huge operation, the quality of wine-making at
Moët is very high, reflecting the innovative excellence of its
technical management and the firm's financial clout in securing
the best grapes. Moët also owns the largest vineyards of any
champagne house – 1,235 acres currently in production – but
these only meet about 20 per cent of the firm's needs.
Remember, a bottle of Moët is uncorked somewhere in the
world every two seconds.

Claude Moët, a broker and grower from the Grande Vallée
de la Marne, founded the business in 1743. But it was really his
grandson, Jean-Rémy Moët, who made it famous through his
friendship with Napoleon. Between 1805 and his death in 1841,
Moët was the most celebrated wine-maker in Europe; the
orders poured in, and the company became the dominant
champagne house. Opposite Moët's offices on Epernay's
Avenue de Champagne stands the Trianon, twin white pavilions
with a formal sunken garden and exquisite orangery, which
Jean-Rémy built to accommodate Napoleon's court on its way
to and from the battlefields of eastern Europe. Now as then,
the Trianon is used to entertain the great and the good.

Trianon Palace in Epernay

Since 1832 the firm has been known as Moët & Chandon, thus incorporating the name of Jean-Rémy's son-in-law, Pierre Gabriel Chandon de Briailles. During the mid-19th century the family became the greatest vineyard owners in Champagne, the list of clients grew longer, and Richard Wagner consoled himself with a bottle of Moët when his opera *Tanhäuser* flopped at its Paris première in 1861. By the last years of the century, Moët & Chandon had about a 16 percent share of the booming export market. The firm then went into a period of decline until it was rescued by Comte Robert-Jean de Voguë in the early 1930s.

Undaunted by the effects of the great depression, de Voguë persuaded his fellow directors to relaunch an unused *marque* called *Dom Pérignon*, bought from Mercier in 1930, as a prestige cuvée for export markets. It was a brilliant marketing coup in view of Moët & Chandon's long-standing ownership of the Abbey and vineyards of Hautvillers and the company's association with the famous monk and champagne-maker. The first shipments arrived in London in 1935 and in New York the following year. *Dom Pérignon* has been the most famous champagne in America ever since. Having survived internment in a German deportation camp, de

Dom Pérignon Rosé 1982

◀ *Dom Pérignon 1985*

Voguë rapidly expanded the firm's sales after the Second World War. By 1962, when Moët became the first champagne house to be quoted on the French *Bourse*, those sales had reached 10 million bottles a year. A period of huge growth followed, with the firm's acquisition of Ruinart (1963), Mercier (1970), and the Christian Dior perfume house (1971). In 1973 the company started its first sparkling wine venture in the New World with its purchase of Domaine Chandon in Napa Valley, California, quickly followed by a second in Brazil 12 months later. Since then it has established its most impressive sparkling wine operation to date (in terms of the really excellent fizz in the bottle) at Domaine Chandon in Australia's Yarra Valley, where since 1985 Dr. Tony Jordan has been fashioning champagne-method wines from classic grapes to rival the real thing. And, the company also produces *Cava* at the Chandon vineyard in Spain's Penedés.

Back home in Epernay, Moët's champagnes at the non-vintage level are once again decent and reliable (after a bad time in the 1970s), and its vintage wines are excellent representatives of the years from which they come. The flagship *Brut Impérial* "White Star" is a bright, firm, fruity wine,

STYLES
NON-VINTAGE
BRUT IMPÉRIAL WHITE STAR DEMI-SEC
VINTAGE
BRUT IMPÉRIAL (1986)
BRUT IMPÉRIAL ROSÉ (1986)
PRESTIGE
DOM PÉRIGNON (1985)
DOM PÉRIGNON ROSÉ (1982)

Brut Impérial ▶

the flavor dominated by black grapes but with a good amount of Chardonnay too; it always seems to improve a lot with a further 12 months in bottle after shipment, and old bottles can be vigorously alive. The *Vintage Brut Impérial* 1986 is a highly distinctive, generously flavored champagne, with notes of spices and brown bread – a typical Moët touch – that comes in part from the 30 percent Pinot Meunier grapes in the blend.

The *Dom Pérignon* 1985, with its highish percentage of Chardonnay supported by extremely ripe Pinot Noir from the firm's own vineyards on the Montagne de Reims and the Grande Vallée de la Marne, is a truly sumptuous yet beautifully balanced wine, the work of Richard Geoffroy, a former medical doctor and one of the finest wine-makers in Champagne. The *Dom Pérignon Rosé* 1982 is another master-piece: it is peach-colored, and its superb expression of fully evolved Chardonnay flavors will delight the most demanding connoisseur. On current showing, both *Dom Pérignon* wines are prestige cuvées that are worth their very high price.

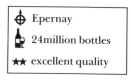

Epernay

24million bottles

★★ excellent quality

*Brut Impériale 1988
Vintage*

*Brut Impériale
Rosé 1986*

Brut Impériale N.V.

*White Star: best-selling
N.V. cuvée in the United States*

JEAN MOUTARDIER

*It is said that when the chef de caves at Veuve Clicquot
starts to compose the blend for his champagnes, he always
sets the Pinot Meunier of Jean Moutardier to
one side as a model by which to judge others.*

*M*outardier is probably the finest exponent of Pinot Meunier-based champagne, his own creations giving the lie to the myth that the finest sparkling wines are always made from Pinot Noir and Chardonnay. He now sells most of his production as finished champagne directly from his 49-acre domaine and modern cellar in Le Breuil, a little village near Dormans. He is ably assisted by his daughters, one of whom, Lily, is married to an Englishman, Jonathan Saxby, who gave up a career as an executive with Rank Hovis McDougall, learned champagne-making at the local wine school in Avize, and is rapidly taking over the business from his father-in-law Jean.

STYLES

NON-VINTAGE
MOUTARDIER CARTE
D'OR

ROSÉ
MOUTARDIER ROSÉ
BRUT

VINTAGE
MOUTARDIER BRUT
RÉSERVE (1986)

PRESTIGE
MOUTARDIER BRUT
SÉLECTION

Carte D'Or ▶

The *Moutardier Brut Réserve* (a vintage wine) is made entirely from Pinot Meunier, a real rarity. The 1986 has a strong, deep gold color and an intense flavor of ripe, red fruit tinged with spice but balanced by excellent acidity. The *Carte d'Or* (non-vintage) is composed of 80 percent Pinot Meunier and is very fruity and full-bodied without being heavy. It is very good value for money. There is also a delicious salmon-colored *Rosé* with a delectable, wild strawberry fruitiness. All these boldly flavored wines, the pink in particular, are excellent matches for Chinese cuisine.

Altogether different is the top-of-the-range *Brut Sélection* which is a classic mix of Pinot Noir and Chardonnay. Subtlety is the keynote, with its nuanced color, delicate *mousse*, and long complex flavor, though this champagne is less *Brut* than many, with quite a high *dosage*.

⊕ Le Breuil

180,000 bottles

★★ excellent quality

|O| Peking duck

Moutardier Rosé Brut

Moutardier Brut Sélection

Moutardier Carte D'Or Brut

Vintage Brut Réserve 1988

G. H. MUMM

Since the early 1950s Cordon Rouge *has been the big champagne name on the American market, and the brand image is so strong that it is still given to several champagnes in the Mumm range, both vintage and non-vintage.*

The firm was founded in 1827 by the brothers Jules, Edouard, and Gottlieb de Mumm and their partner, M. Giesler. The brothers Mumm, German Protestants, came from Rüdesheim on the Rheingau, where they had owned vineyards and an important wine distribution business. In 1838, G. H. Mumm, Gottlieb's son, joined the company and in 1853 it took his name. For the next 50 years, the Mumms owned and managed the firm, but they remained German citizens. As a result, on the outbreak of the First World War in 1914, the firm's assets and vineyards were confiscated

⊕ Reims

🍾 10.8 million bottles

★ good quality

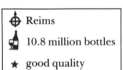

Mumm de Cramant

Cordon Rouge Brut N.V.: leading champagne brand in the United States ▶

by the French government; in 1920 G. H. Mumm and Co., then the largest champagne company in Reims, was put up for sale by auction and bought by the *Societé Vinicole de Champagne Successeurs*. In 1955, the Canadian-based Seagram group acquired an interest in Mumm, later a controlling one, and the company is now part of a huge, international drinks conglomerate.

Mumm's flagship brand, *Cordon Rouge*, is probably more famous than the name of the firm. *Cordon Rouge* was first introduced in 1875 by Mumm's Paris agent, who had the bright idea of decorating the bottle with the sash of the *Legion d'Honneur* in order to boost sales. The ribbon was later abandoned in favor of a label inscribed with the words *Cordon Rouge* on a wide diagonal red stripe, and was only resuscitated in 1991 with the launch of the firm's new prestige cuvée, the 1985 *Mumm Grand Cordon Rouge*, which was decorated with a reproduction of the *Legion d'Honneur* ribbon.

The range and style of the champagnes on the Cordon Rouge label is, too diverse to give an accurate general description, but how good are the

Cordon Vert Demi-Sec

◀ *René Lalou Prestige Cuvée*

individual wines from this major champagne player?

The hugely successful non-vintage *Cordon Rouge Brut* has received mixed, sometimes downright hostile, reviews from the pundits. In December 1990 the French magazine *Que Choisir* wrote that it was "very little appreciated, (with) too large bubbles, a powerful but unbalanced nose, too much acidity for certain tasters and not enough length." My own impression of this cuvée (tasted in December 1993) was of a fresh, fruity wine in a green rather immature style, artfully rounded out to a just off-dry flavor by the use of a slightly higher than average *dosage* than is usually the case with a truly *Brut* Champagne. It is a decent but unexciting product, fully priced, and is relatively poor value for money. Its blend is a conventional mix of all three champagne grapes. *Cordon Vert* (also non-vintage) is a rich champagne, officially classified as *Demi-Sec*, soft, round, but really quite sweet.

Mumm de Cramant is a rare wine made from different vintages of Chardonnay grapes from the village of Cramant, rated 100 percent on the *échelle de cru*. Of lovely citron color, the wine sparkles

Cordon Rouge 1985 Vintage

Mumm de Cramant Blanc de Blancs: 100% Chardonnay Champagne from the village of Cramant ▶

gently; the taste is dry, ultra-pure, and fresh, with lemon and butter notes. It is, however, a very light wine and finishes too short for my liking. *Cordon Rouge* 1985 is a fine vintage wine (70 percent Pinot Noir, 30 percent Chardonnay), with a nutty nose and a nice touch of maturity. *Cordon Rouge Rosé* 1985 is of similar composition to the vintage *Cordon Rouge*; the color is a deep blush, and there is a whiff of soft red fruit, which is confirmed on the palate – an excellent rosé by any standard. The two Mumm prestige cuvées are also first-rate, and so they should be as they are very expensive: *René Lalou* 1985, reputedly the favorite bubbly of H.M. Queen Elizabeth the Queen Mother, is a big champagne (50 percent Pinot Noir, 50 percent Chardonnay), ripe-tasting with no hint of austerity; *Grand Cordon Rouge* 1985, the star of the range, is subtle but steely with a seemingly dominant Chardonnay character (actually 50 percent of the blend) that is shaped by the best Côte des Blancs grapes from Cramant and Avize; the big aftertaste, though, shows the intensity of *grand cru* Pinot Noir which makes up the other half of the blend.

STYLES

NON-VINTAGE

CUVÉE CORDON ROUGE

CUVÉE CORDON VERT,
DEMI-SEC

VINTAGE

CORDON ROUGE (1985)

CORDON ROUGE ROSÉ

(1985)

PRESTIGE

RENÉ LALOU (1985)

GRAND CORDON
ROUGE (1985)

MUMM DE CRAMANT

René Lalou 1985 Prestige　　*Grand Cordon 1985 (Prestige)*

NAPOLÉON

*Don't be deceived by the staid labels or the old-fashioned
premises, where a visit is like a walk through time, for
Napoléon champagnes are always good
and sometimes superb.*

This little gem of a firm in **Vertus** at the
southern end of the Côte des Blancs,
founded in 1825, is really called Ch. & A. Prieur,
after the sons of the founder. In 1898 the third
generation of the family managed to register
the name Napoléon as a *marque* and shipped a
small quantity of champagne to **Russia**. The
standard non-vintage *Napoléon Carte Verte Brut*
is usually made from three-quarters Pinot
Meunier and a quarter Chardonnay; light
and clean-flavored, it is for early drinking.
The *Napoléon Tradition Carte d'Or*, despite
its kitsch label, is a wonderful champagne;
Chardonnay, while only accounting for
about 40 percent of the blend, shapes
the wine's elegance and lovely balance,
but there is real richness here too from
Pinot Noir — the nicest surprise I experienced with any champagne while
researching this book. The 1985
Vintage Brut tastes remarkably like
the *Carte d'Or*. Are they by chance re-
lated? Until 1994, the firm, still run
by the Prieur family, was the smallest
grande marque house, but it resigned
because it could no longer afford the
fees to finance that club's promotional
ambitions.

*Napoléon Tradition Carte D'Or
Brut: an excellent traditional
champagne* ▶

STYLES	
NON-VINTAGE	**VINTAGE**
NAPOLÉON CARTE VERTE BRUT	NAPOLÉON VINTAGE BRUT (1985)
NAPOLÉON TRADITION CARTE D'OR BRUT	

Napoléon Carte Verte Brut

Vintage 1973

 Vertus

160,000 bottles

★★ excellent quality

Étienne Prieur of Champagne Napoléon

BRUNO PAILLARD

Bruno specializes in very dry, deep flavored champagnes with minimal dosage. *His vintage wines are dressed with chic labels illustrated by prominent artists, and carry the date of disgorging.*

ounded in 1981 by a dynamic young broker, Bruno Paillard, the firm is now installed in a sleek, modern winery on the southern outskirts of Reims. Eighty percent of the firm's production is exported, mainly to the United States, Great Britain, Belgium, and Switzerland.

Strongly flavored as they undoubtedly are, Paillard champagnes also have considerable finesse. As its name implies, the

Reims
350,000 bottles
★★ excellent quality

Première Cuvée Brut Rosé

Première Cuvée Brut

Chardonnay Réserve Privée

non-vintage *Première Cuvée Brut* is made from the first pressings of all three champagne grapes. Of vivid gold color with a fine *mousse*, this is a fresh, definitely dry champagne at once fruity and vinous with exemplary persistence of flavor. The *Première Cuvée Rosé* has a translucent light-salmon hue, the nose is floral and Chardonnayesque, the palate Pinotesque, powerful yet fine and restrained – one of the best rosés around. The *Chardonnay Réserve Privée* is a distinctive wine, its whiff of toast and vanilla suggesting that a proportion of the wines in the blend were fermented in wood; the taste is all lemony delicacy and bone-dry. The *Vintage Brut* 1985 has a rich, evolved flavor with a lovely note of ripe Chardonnay, typical of this great year.

Brut 1985

STYLES

NON-VINTAGE
PREMIÈRE CUVÉE BRUT
CHARDONNAY
RÉSERVE PRIVÉE
ROSÉ
PREMIÈRE CUVÉE ROSÉ
VINTAGE
VINTAGE BRUT (1985)

◀ *Blanc de Blancs Chardonnay Brut: incisive, well-defined Chardonnay champagne*

PALMER & CO

---

*Palmer is one of the best cooperatives in Champagne and
one small enough to concentrate on quality.*

P almer's 180 member-growers cultivate 778 acres of
mainly *premier cru* Pinot Noir grapes on the Montagne de
Reims. There are no short-cuts in the wine-making, which takes
place in a modern *cuverie* above old, deep cellars in the center
of Reims. Processes like *remuage* are given plenty of time to
achieve the best results. The champagnes are made with at
least 20 percent reserve wines and they are rested for three to
six months after *dégorgement*.

Most unusually for a cooperative, Palmer has a "library" of
older vintages from 1979 back to 1947. A bottle of the 1961
shared with the ebullient director Jean-Claude Colson in
January 1994 was a magnificent, old champagne which still
tasted as fresh as a daisy.

Brut 1985

Brut N.V.

Brut Cuvée Rubis Rosé

Of the regular range, the standard *Brut* (non-vintage), made from equal parts of Pinot Noir and Chardonnay, is a lot better than many flagship wines from the *grandes marques*; fresh, elegant and of real complexity. The *Rosé Brut* is a full-flavored expression of Pinot Noir, while the 1982 *Blanc de Blancs* is drinking at the peak of its maturity, but will keep well in a cool cellar until 1995–96.

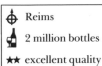

⊕ Reims

🍾 2 million bottles

★★ excellent quality

STYLES

NON-VINTAGE

BRUT

ROSÉ

ROSÉ BRUT

VINTAGE

BLANC DE BLANCS (1982)

Jean Claude Colson of Champagne Palmer

◀ *Non-vintage Brut: a well-aged champagne of real complexity*

PANNIER

Pannier specializes in wines based on Pinot Meunier that are immaculately vinified to produce flattering, fruit-driven champagnes offering excellent value for money.

his group of growers at Château Thierry farms 1,013 acres mainly in the Vallée de la Marne but have access to grapes from the Montagne de Reims and the Côte des Blancs. *Tradition Brut*, with more than 50 percent Pinot Meunier, has an inviting, pale yet vital color, a fine, persistent *mousse*, clear fruit definition, and a supple yet vinous flavor. The prestige cuvée, *Égerie de Pannier* can be a memorable bottle; Chardonnay adds refinement and a toasty scent. The opulent 1985 *Égerie* has been replaced by the 1988, which should be kept until 1995.

⊕	Château Thierry
🍾	1 million bottles
★	good quality

STYLES

NON-VINTAGE

TRADITION BRUT

ROSÉ

BRUT ROSÉ

VINTAGE

VINTAGE BRUT (1988)

PRESTIGE

ÉGERIE DE PANNIER
(1985, 1988)

Tradition Brut ▶

PERRIER-JOUËT

*Perrier-Jouët has always been one of the most prestigious
champagne houses. Its superb vineyards at Avize and
neighboring Cramant account for the hazelnut aromas
and creamy flavors of top-flight Chardonnay that are so
typical of Perrier-Jouët vintage champagnes.*

Founded in 1811 by Pierre Nicolas-Marie Perrier, who
had married Adèle Jouët, Perrier-Jouët quickly became
known in the English-speaking world: its first shipments of
champagne were dispatched to Great Britain in 1815 and to
the United States in 1837. Pierre's son, Charles Perrier, was a
deft politician and a famous Mayor of Epernay who built the
grandiose Château Perrier opposite the firm's elegant premises
in the Avenue de Champagne. It now houses the town library
and museum and is well worth a visit. Charles Perrier greatly
expanded the firm's exports to Great Britain, and by the time
of his death in 1897, P.J. (as it was nicknamed) numbered
among its devotees women as different as Queen Victoria and
the actress Sarah Bernhardt, who reputedly liked to bathe in
its wines.

Charles Perrier had no children but the firm passed into the
safe hands of his nephew, Henry Gallice, who was an important
figure in the fight against phylloxera in the Champagne region
during the early 1900s. In 1934, Perrier-Jouët was acquired by
Louis Budin, who had married a Gallice. His son Michel became
managing director in 1959, the same year that Mumm Champagne (later to be owned by the Seagram group) took a majority
shareholding in the company. Budin, a very fine taster, was
wisely allowed to go on making the excellent type of champagne

1988 Perrier-Jouët Brut

which had established the high reputation of the house in the 19th century. Budin's greatest coup, both aesthetically and commercially, was his launch in 1970 of the firm's distinctive flower-decorated prestige cuvée *Belle Epoque*. Budin's choice of venue and occasion was inspired: a Paris nightclub to celebrate the 70th birthday of the American jazz musician Duke Ellington; at a stroke P.J.'s *grande marque* image was strongly reinforced in the United States, where by 1987 it had become the third largest champagne brand.

P.J.'s major assets are its 247 acres of vineyards, especially the superb Chardonnay sites on the Côte des Blancs. The firm owns 67 acres in Avize alone, and 22 acres at Cramant. The house's other vineyards include 22 acres at Mailly-Champagne on the Montagne de Reims, 49 acres at Dizy and Ay in the Grande Vallée de la Marne, and a sizeable 78 acres of Pinot Meunier at Vinay and Orbais. Nevertheless the company still buys in about 60 percent of its grape needs.

STYLES
NON-VINTAGE
GRAND BRUT
BLASON DE FRANCE BRUT
ROSÉ
BLASON DE FRANCE BRUT ROSÉ
VINTAGE
RÉSERVE CUVÉE BRUT (1985)
PRESTIGE
BELLE EPOQUE BRUT (1985)

Belle Epoque 1985: in its famous, flower-decorated bottle ▶

The non-vintage *Grand Brut* is made from all three champagne grape varieties but is dominated by the two Pinots, which give the wine a chunky, meaty style. The *Blason de France Brut* is altogether finer; the better-class grapes in the blend and the longer time in bottle produce a champagne with an evolved, yeasty, complex nose and a poised richness on the palate – a classy bottle. The *Blason de France Brut Rosé* is an excellent well-aged cuvée; rose-colored with brick and orange tints, the black fruit and grilled bread aromas soar out of the glass, while the Pinot flavors are mouth-enveloping and persistent. The *Vintage Réserve Cuvée Brut* 1985 is a classic example of the P.J. vintage style with its nutty, creamy Chardonnay character – class in a glass, and what great champagne is all about. The *Belle Epoque Brut* 1985 is one of the finest champagnes I have ever drunk; a 50/50 Pinot Noir–Chardonnay blend, this wine has everything: supreme elegance, aromas of flowers, a toasty richness, and terrific complexity. Each time I taste it I discover new flavors.

⊕	Epernay
🍾	3 million cases
★★	excellent quality

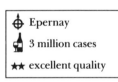

Blason de France Brut

◀ *Perrier-Jouët Grand Brut N.V.*

JOSEPH PERRIER

*Off the beaten track in Châlons-sur-Marne,
Joseph Perrier is one of the hidden jewels of the
champagne world.*

Thanks to its low profile, this small *grande marque* house, founded in 1825, has been left in peace to make mellow, fruit-laden champagnes whose price has not yet caught up with their quality. The ripe, generous house style comes from the sunny location of the firm's 49 acres of Pinot Noir and Pinot Meunier vineyards at Cumières, Damery, and Hautvillers.

The non-vintage *Cuvée Royale Brut* is consistently pleasurable. Straw-gold in color and made from one-third Chardonnay and two-thirds black grapes, it has an expansive smell of raspberries and a broad, spicy flavor; mellow too, with at least three years' bottle age. The vintage 1985 *Brut* is paler, more refined, and with a classy taste of citrus fruit (45 percent Chardonnay in this blend). The firm has wisely decided to go on to the excellent 1989 vintage for release in early 1995, by which time the 1985 will be sold out. The *Rosé Brut* is strictly for those who like a full

Blanc de Blancs

Cuvée Royale

Cuvée Royale 1985

Brut Rosé

fruit style, since this wine is pervaded with the taste of cherries and raspberries. The real star here is the *Cuvée de Luxe Josephine* 1985, a true three-star champagne and a wonderful expression of ripe, mature Chardonnay that, although accounting for only half the blend, dominates the wine's flavor.

⊕ Châlons-sur-Marne

🍾 650,000 bottles

★★ excellent quality

STYLES

NON-VINTAGE
CUVÉE ROYALE BRUT

ROSÉ
ROSÉ BRUT

VINTAGE
CUVÉE ROYALE
VINTAGE BRUT (1985)

PRESTIGE
CUVÉE DE LUXE
JOSEPHINE (1985)

Chef de caves at Joseph Perrier

◀ *Cuvée Josephine 1985*

PHILIPPONNAT

*A small traditional firm which deserves to be better
known, Philipponnat makes champagnes for the
true connoisseur.*

This house was founded in 1910, although the family have
been growers in the Vallée de la Marne since the end of the
17th century. Philipponnat's prize possession is the 13-acre Clos
des Goisses at Mareuil, the largest walled vineyard in Champagne. Across the board, their champagnes are wines of vinosity and character, delicate and gently sparkling, with a high
proportion of reserve wines in the blends.

The non-vintage *Royale Réserve Brut*, made from 70 percent
black grapes and 30 percent Chardonnay (one-fifth of the total
being reserve wines), is an admirable flagship champagne,
mellow yet with well-defined, sprightly fruit and a classically
dry, clean finish. Dominated by 70 percent Pinot Noir, this
champagne is made by highly traditional methods including a
first fermentation in wooden casks. The result in the 1986

Royale Réserve Brut

Brut 1986 Réserve Speciale

Clos de Goisses

vintage (very difficult elsewhere) is first-rate, with an impressive ripeness and concentration (a true three-star champagne). The more recent *Le Reflet* cuvée is a classic mix of Chardonnay and Pinot Noir, the latter grapes coming from the Clos des Goisses. The honeysuckle aromas and brisk acidity of Chardonnay characterize this wine, which would make a fine partner for that greatest of deep-water fish, the sea bass. Philipponnat has been owned since 1987 by the Marie Brizard family-run drinks group.

 Mareuil-sur-Ay

 500,000 bottles

★★ excellent quality

 Le Reflet with roasted sea-bass

STYLES

NON-VINTAGE

ROYALE RÉSERVE BRUT

ROSÉ

ROSÉ BRUT

VINTAGE

CLOS DES GOISSES (1986)

LE REFLET

Le Reflet

◀ *Royale Réserve Brut*

PLOYEZ-JACQUEMART

Wine-making by this "boutique" champagne firm is traditional. The prise de mousse takes place in deep cellars, and the champagnes are given plenty of bottle age.

Gérard Ployez and his daughter Laurence own a vineyard at Ludes and Mailly-Champagne, but buy in most of their grapes from highly rated *crus* in the Côte des Blancs and the Vallée de la Marne. Chardonnay accounts for at least 50 percent of the blend – and more in exceptional years. The range includes a rich, well-rounded *Extra Quality Brut*, an exceptional *Blanc de Blancs* 1985 and a barrel-fermented prestige *Cuvée Liesse* d'Harbonville.

 Ludes

🍾 80,000 bottles

★ good quality

STYLES

NON-VINTAGE

EXTRA QUALITY BRUT

VINTAGE

GRANDE RÉSERVE SÉLECTION

BLANC DE BLANCS (1985)

PRESTIGE

CUVÉE LIESSE D'HARBONVILLE (1985)

Extra Quality Brut ▶

POL ROGER

*For consistently pleasurable champagnes, the house of
Pol Roger has few equals. I have never drunk a
disappointing bottle from this model family firm, which
says a lot about the people behind the label.*

hristian de Billy and Christian Pol-Roger, great grandsons
of the founder, are totally committed to the highest standards
of quality, and they have never been tempted to overexpand
this smallish *grande marque* or to diversify into other wine-
making ventures. The cousins simply make sure that the firm
sticks to classic precepts of champagne-making, yet a lightness
of touch is reflected in their wines, which are among the most
subtle, *nuancé*, and delicious in the region.

The house was founded in 1849 by Pol Roger, a native of
Ay. In 1876 he shipped his first champagnes to England, which
was to become the firm's major market. It was his son Maurice
Pol-Roger who really made the brand famous. He was an out-
standingly brave mayor of Epernay during the German occupation of the town in 1914. By 1935 he had established the
champagne as the number one in Great Britain, which was a
pretty remarkable achievement for a small quality-first house.
Maurice was also a great hunter and fisherman. His tastes in
champagne were as robust as his field pursuits, for during his
time the wines were dominated by Pinot Noir: he seemed to
have little love for Chardonnay, which he described as *"la*

Maison Pol Roger in Epernay

flotte" (water). The big bouncy flavors of old-style Pol Roger clearly appealed to Winston Churchill, who became the brand's greatest fan. His loyalty to the house was strengthened by his friendship with Odette Pol-Roger, Maurice's daughter-in-law, an Anglophile, after whom he named one of his racing fillies.

Pol Roger champagnes are now much more Chardonnayesque in flavor, the style shaped by the 198 acres of vineyards around Epernay and along the northern *Côte des Blancs*, which the firm started to acquire in the mid-1950s. Several of these vineyards – especially those in Mardeuil, Epernay, Pierry, Cuis, and Chouilly – produce, I reckon, quite forward, beautifully fragrant wines, which is the quintessential P.R. touch. The wines are also extremely fresh but age exceptionally well, thanks to the firm's excellent *chef de caves* James Coffinet who used to work for Billecart-Salmon.

The non-vintage *White Foil* is a classic *assemblage* of all three champagne grapes in equal proportions. It is a fine example of the house style, light but structured, fresh yet ripe and fruity, and ready to drink. The *Sec* is of identical composition but with a slightly higher *dosage*. The vintage 1986 *Extra Dry* is a 60/40 mix of Pinot Noir and Chardonnay, the latter dominating the aromas but with a big expansive Pinot flavor and a very long finish. The vintage-dated *Blanc de Chardonnay* is usually one of the most beguiling *blanc de blancs* on the market. The 1985 was a lovely wine of lace-like delicacy with aromas of hawthorn; the

⊕ Epernay

🍾 1.4 million bottles

★★ the best quality available

Pol Roger White Foil ▶

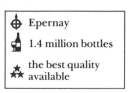

1986 initially looked less impressive but at a recent tasting (March 1994) blossomed into a champagne of refined richness. The vintage-dated *Rosé* is also worth seeking out; light salmon-pink in color, it has a positive Pinotesque red fruit smell but is "lifted" by a good proportion of Chardonnay. At the top of the range there are two prestige cuvées. The *Réserve Speciale P.R.* 1986 is made from equal parts of Pinot Noir and Chardonnay from six *grands crus*; a wine of finesse, depth and real complexity. The grape composition of the *Cuvée Sir Winston Churchill* is not disclosed but it is almost certainly greatly dominated by Pinot Noir (as much as 70 or 80 percent, perhaps). This is a very big champagne of which the old war lord would have certainly approved. Some tasters note a delicacy and smell of lilacs in the 1985 vintage; I am more struck by its power and the need to keep it until 1997–98.

STYLES

NON-VINTAGE

WHITE FOIL

SEC

ROSÉ

VINTAGE ROSÉ (1986)

VINTAGE

VINTAGE EXTRA DRY
(1986)

BLANC DE
CHARDONNAY (1986)

PRESTIGE

CUVÉE SIR WINSTON
CHURCHILL (1985)
RÉSERVE SPÉCIALE PR
(1986)

Presentation Box: Pol Roger Cuvée PR Prestige

Brut Rosé 1986

Blanc de Chardonnay 1986

Extra Dry 1986

Brut 1985

Christian de Billy, President of Pol Roger

P O M M E R Y

Pommery is the sleeping giant of the champagne world, a
firm with a fascinating past but one which has never
quite realized its full potential in the post-1945 world.

ounded in 1836, the firm achieved greatness under a
famous champagne widow, Louise Pommery, who took
control on the death of her husband in 1858. *"Qualité d'abord"*
("Quality first") was Madame Pommery's motto. She decided
to concentrate on the English market. Her intention was to
produce champagne in as delicate, fine, and dry a style as possible. Her legendary 1874 vintage, which took Victorian London
by storm, was the first genuinely *brut* or dry champagne as we
would understand the term, with a *dosage* of just 6–9 grams of
sugar per liter.

Madame Pommery's boldest move was the acquisition of a
large area of land on the outskirts of Reims covering 120 Roman
chalk pits. Above these she built a series of hideous edifices,
their design based, it is said, on the baronial mansions of her
aristocratic English customers. The Roman pits below she used
as storage cellars, decorating them with beautiful sculpted bas-
reliefs, all connected by a network of 11 miles of galleries and
passages. These magnificent cellars can be visited every day of
the week. American visitors will be interested in the splendid
carved blending cask in the reception hall, with a capacity of
100,000 bottles, which was sent by the firm to St. Louis, Missouri,

A selection of champagnes from a famous
grand-marque house

for the Universal Fair of 1904. The carved figures on the cask depict Franco-American friendship.

Pommery's 759 acres of vineyards are among the largest of any firm's in Champagne. There are particularly fine ones on the Montagne de Reims. Nearly every *cru* has a 100 percent *echelle de cru* rating. Yet these only account for about one-third of the firm's needs. And since L.V.M.H. acquired Pommery in 1990, the company has decided to go for volume sales, hoping to reach 8 million bottles a year by 1996. This will make it less dependent on the magnificent vineyards which are the firm's greatest assets and source of profit. A sure-fire way, some might say, of killing a brand.

Worrying as this trend is, in fairness I have to say that Pommery's wines have improved in recent years, thanks to its talented *chef de caves*, Prince Alain de Polignac. The *Brut Royal* (non-vintage), a classic mix of Pinot Noir, Chardonnay, and Pinot Meunier, is an intricate assembly of 30 to 40 *crus* with a good amount (20 percent) of reserve wines in the blend. Released after three to four years in the bottle, it is a friendly, easy-drinking champagne of broad fruitiness, though the *dosage* seems quite high. The *Vintage Brut* 1988 (60 percent Chardonnay, 50 percent Pinot Noir) is a fine, delicate wine with real purity of fruit – a de Polignac signature – while the prestige *Cuvée Louise Pommery* 1985 is first-rate. It is sourced from the firm's *grand cru* holdings in Cramant and Avize for Chardonnay,

⊕	Reims
🍾	6 million bottles
★	good quality

Brut Royale N.V. ▶

Cuvée Spéciale 1985

Rosé 1988

Vintage 1988 Rosé

Pommery Rosé N.V.

Pommery Brut Royal N.V.

Brut Royale N.V.

Brut 1988

and Ay for Pinot Noir. It has a lovely floral note on the nose, and in the mouth is rich, and long-flavored, but perfectly balanced. This is a house capable of achieving a two-star rating, though a question mark must hang over future quality in view of its over-rapid sales growth.

Carved blending vat sent to St. Louis, Missouri, for the Universal Fair of 1904

STYLES

NON-VINTAGE

BRUT ROYAL

VINTAGE

VINTAGE BRUT (1988)

PRESTIGE

CUVÉE LOUISE POMMERY (1987, 1985)

LOUISE POMMERY ROSÉ (1988)

Louise Pommery 1985: the label depicts the famous champagne widow ▶

ALAIN ROBERT

Le Mesnil-sur-Oger — site of Alain Robert's grand cru
*vineyards — is probably the best village on the Côte des
Blancs for making* Blanc de Blancs *champagne.*

Alain Robert is the current head of an
old family of growers who came to Le
Mesnil in the 17th century. He owns 30 acres of
grand cru vineyards in seven villages of the Côte
des Blancs. Robert's champagnes are made
entirely from Chardonnay, and though they
do not carry a vintage year they are, in fact,
wines from a single year. The *Blanc de Blancs
Brut* is a blend of wines from his vineyards in
the 1985 vintage; it has lots of Chardonnay
character and a nice touch of maturity, but
lacks a little finesse. The *Blanc de Blancs
Sélection* (1986 vintage) is finer and more
delicate and comes from Robert's better
vineyards. *Le Mesnil* (1982) strikes a
perfect balance between mellow richness and exquisite elegance. *Blanc de
Blancs* champagne does not come any
better than this.

⊕ Le Mesnil-sur-Oger

🍾 100,000 bottles

★★ excellent quality

🍽 poached salmon
with sorrel sauce

*Alain Robert Brut
Sélection: a high quality
Blanc de Blancs* ▶

STYLES

VINTAGE	PRESTIGE
BLANC DE BLANCS BRUT	BLANC DE BLANCS, LE MESNIL
BLANC DE BLANCS SÉLECTION	

TÊTE
1979
DE
CUVÉE

Tête de Cuvée 1979

"Vieux dosé"

Vieux Dosé: the dosage was added early in the production process

Blanc de Blancs

Blanc de Blancs Brut

Blanc de Blancs Sélection

Le Mesnil Brut Rare 1978 ▶

LOUIS ROEDERER

*Louis Roederer is a very great champagne house and also
one of the most profitable. Its great brand,* Cristal, *is
probably the most sought-after prestige cuvée in the
world at the moment.*

R oederer's high reputation and financial soundness rest on
a near self-sufficiency in grapes from its 445 acres of
vineyards, controlled sales, and its one great brand.

The first Louis Roederer, who was born in Alsace, joined
his uncle's champagne business at Reims in 1827, and six years
later inherited the firm. Young Louis's early prospecting of
foreign markets paid dividends. By the time of his death in
1870, the firm had become the third largest shipper of champagne to the United States, and it was soon to challenge Veuve
Clicquot's dominance of the Russian market. For in 1876, at
the request of Czar Alexander II, the now famous *Cristal* was
specially created to satisfy the imperial sweet tooth. It was
presented in a clear lead-crystal bottle exclusively for Alexander's use. With the October Revolution of 1917, the firm's
Russian market collapsed, but its fortunes were revived in 1932
by another of the industry's strong-willed widows, Camille Olry-

A pannier presentation of Louis Roederer Brut Premier

Roederer, who led the company for 42 years and developed the brand very successfully with unusual showmanship. While she was looking for a new market, she would enter one of her champion trotters in a race and then throw a lavish victory party afterwards. The name of her champagne would be on everyone's lips for months. It was Madame Roederer who shrewdly bought the firm's vineyards in the 1930s. She died in 1975, leaving the company to her daughter, Madame Claude Rouzaud. It is now run by her grandson, Jean-Claude, a trained oenologist and proud of it.

Jean-Claude is a perfectionist, for whom the wine is more important than the bubbles. He restricted the amount of champagne produced because he wanted as much control as possible over the grapes. "Seventy percent of the quality of our wines comes from our own vineyards," he says, "so if you have to buy in poor grapes, you often have to grip the table when you drink the finished champagne."

The Roederer vineyards are exceptionally well sited (averaging 98 percent on the *échelle de cru*) and intelligently spread across the three classic champagne districts: on the Montagne de Reims at Ay, Verzenay, Verzy, and Louvois; in the Haute Vallée de la Marne at Cumières and Hautvillers; and on the Côte des Blancs at Chouilly, Cramant, Avize, Le Mesnil, and Vertus. In the cellars at Reims, the attention to the smaller details of fine wine-making is very impressive. All the wines are fermented in

⊕ Reims

🍾 2 million bottles

★★ the best quality available

Louis Roederer Brut Premier ▶

STYLES	
NON-VINTAGE	**VINTAGE**
BRUT PREMIER	VINTAGE BRUT (1986)
ROSÉ	CRISTAL VINTAGE
ROSÉ BRUT	BRUT (1988)

Jean-Claude Rouzaud:
head of Louis Roederer

Roederer Cristal 1986

Brut Premier

◀ *Roederer Cristal*

stainless steel vats of small capacity so that the flavor and individuality of each *cru* may be better shaped. The really distinguishing feature here is the use of large oak barrels *(foudres)* to age the reserve wines, for it is the spell in wood that gives Roederer champagnes their honeyed vanilla taste.

The *Brut Premier* is an upmarket non-vintage champagne, aged for longer than usual (three to four years) and intended to give immediate pleasure on release; its red fruit flavor dominated by Pinot Noir (66 percent) has flattering vanilla scents coming from about 20 percent wood-aged reserve wines. *Vintage Brut* 1986 is probably the best-made *grande marque* champagne from that difficult year; unlike a lot of the competition, it has real structure and an "animal" Pinot character. The *Rosé* is one of the most distinctive around: made from Pinot Noir grapes that have been put in contact with the juice, it has a very light salmon color that belies its rich vinous flavor and makes an excellent match for sautéed kidneys. The newly released *Cristal Vintage Brut* 1988 is a worthy successor to the 1985; a dry wine these days, it has a lovely toasty flavor, the fruit definition is exceptionally fine and really deserves keeping until 1995 before pulling the cork. In the cool Anderson Valley of Northern California, Rouzaud's Roederer Estate has produced a stunningly good sparkling wine called *L'Ermitage* from the best 1989 cuvées.

Louis Roederer Cristal stored in pupitres

RUINART

---

*This, the oldest champagne house, was founded in 1729
by Nicolas Ruinart, a linen merchant and nephew of
Dom Thierry Ruinart, a well-known wine-maker and
colleague of Dom Pérignon.*

The firm prospered through the politically turbulent Napoleonic era, though the family's royalist sympathies were made clear when Irenée Ruinart, as mayor of Reims and deputé for the Marne, welcomed Charles X to his coronation at Reims Cathedral in 1825. Irenée's son, Edmond Ruinart, was an early prospector of the American market. He was received in 1832 by President Jackson, to whom he presented a case of Ruinart champagne. Nearly 30 years later his heir, Edgar, was traveling to Russia where he had an audience with the Czar.

Thanks to adventurous men like the Ruinarts, the total exports of champagne quadrupled between 1850 and 1899. During the First World War the firm's premises in Reims were all but destroyed. Undaunted, André Ruinart, then head of the firm, set up an office in one of his Roman chalk cellars and, when this was badly flooded, installed his working desk on a raft so that business could continue as usual. The house remained a family affair until it was bought by Moët & Chandon in 1963.

Of the great champagne houses, Ruinart has perhaps the lowest profile, for this is a brand known essentially to connoisseurs and is distributed on a very selective basis to fine restaurants and speciality wine and food shops. The premises, restored to their austere 18th-century style, ooze tradition, and the firm's Gallo-Roman chalk cellars (known as "Crayères") are the finest in Reims and classified as a national monument. Every two years the Crayères are the dramatic venue for the presentation of the Trophée Ruinart, the prize in a prestigious international competition to find Europe's best wine steward.

Ruinart champagnes are especially fine and elegant, but they have a mouth-filling richness, and body too, because this is a Chardonnay house of a very particular type. The firm owns 37 acres on the eastern side of the Montagne de Reims, chiefly at Sillery and Puissieulx. The Chardonnay grapes grown in these vineyards have much more power and "flesh" than those from the Côte des Blancs; hence the richness in the wines, especially at the higher end of the range.

Jean-François Barat, Ruinart's *chef de caves*, is a very clear-headed and articulate wine-maker. The exceptionally high standards he has achieved rest on the fundamental notion of intricate blending, a compact range of just five cuvées, a low *dosage* in the finished champagnes, and important stocks of reserve wines.

The non-vintage *"R" de Ruinart* (45 percent Chardonnay, 55 percent Pinot Noir) has four years' bottle age and a fine, gentle *mousse*; there is no fizzy aggression on the nose, just fine floral notes; and it is very supple and easy to drink but with real persistence of flavor thanks to a lot of *premier cru* grapes in the blend. The *"R" de Ruinart* vintage 1988 (50 percent Chardonnay, 50 percent Pinot Noir) is a yellow-gold color with a typically ripe, evolved nose touched with lemon, but with more complex secondary aromas too. All the power and vinosity on the palate is shaped by the presence of 100 percent *échelle de cru* Pinot Noir grapes from the Montagne de Reims. This is a wine with enough character to match a sauced fish dish.

⊕	Reims
🍾	1.5 million bottles
★★	the best quality available
🍽	roasted baby lobster with vanilla sauce

"R" de Ruinart Brut ▶

The prestige cuvée *Dom Ruinart* is one of the best two or three *Blancs de Blancs* on the market. It is made from 100 percent Chardonnay, of which 30 percent comes from the lower slopes of Sillery and Puissieulx. As Jean-François said of the 1986 Dom Ruinart when I tasted it with him, "this wine has the power and body of Pinot Noir in a Chardonnay." It is also wonderfully buttery and fat but extremely elegant. The *Dom Ruinart Rosé* 1985 is for me the finest pink champagne currently on the market. It is made from exactly the same Chardonnay provenances as the *Blanc de Blancs*, but with 20 percent Bouzy Rouge added. It has an extraordinary bouquet, almost Burgundian in its sensual appeal, elegant yet ripe and evolved with tertiary woodland smells, and a wonderfully complex flavor. If it weren't for the bubbles, you might be drinking something very grand from the Côte d'Or. The standard *"R" de Ruinart Rosé* (non-vintage) is in a very different style, more strongly colored and with a simple but agreeable red fruit flavor. It is the only champagne in the current Ruinart range to be made with a proportion of Pinot Meunier grapes.

Jean-François Barot, chef de caves at Ruinart

STYLES

NON-VINTAGE	VINTAGE
"R" DE RUINART	"R" DE RUINART VINTAGE (1988)
ROSÉ	PRESTIGE
"R" DE RUINART ROSÉ	DOM RUINART BLANC DE BLANCS (1986)

"R" de Ruinart Rosé

"R" de Ruinart 1988

"R" de Ruinart Brut N.V.

Dom Ruinart Blanc de Blancs 1985 Prestige Cuvée ▶

SALON

---

*Salon is a story of perfectionism. It is the only house to
produce just one type of champagne, always a* Blanc de
Blancs, *always vintage-dated, and only released in years
when the* chef de caves *thinks the wine is worthy
of the label.*

*T*he *marque* was the creation of Eugène Aimé Salon, a
Champenois born in the tiny village of Pocancy on the plains
east of Le Mesnil-sur-Oger in 1867. Aimé learned the art of
champagne-making as a boy, but he became a teacher and
later a successful furrier and politician in Paris. He was one of
the greatest gourmets of his day, a member of that ultimate
dining club, the Club des Cents, and an habitué Chez Maxim's
where he had a table permanently reserved.

In 1911 Aimé bought a vineyard in Le Mesnil-sur-Oger so
that he could create the perfect champagne made exclusively
from Chardonnay grapes grown in that greatest *cru* of the
Côte des Blancs. At first, Aimé's own champagne was a hobby;
he would offer it unlabelled to his country guests at Pocancy.
But demand for this sensational wine became so strong that
Aimé decided to commercialize it, and Salon was born. Aimé
began to buy grapes from other vignerons in Le Mesnil. Only
the healthiest grapes were used for his champagnes, which
were made entirely from the first pressings and in exceptional
vintages. Grapes and years not thought up to scratch were sold
off to other merchants.

Salon Cuvée "S" 1982: an exceptionally rich vintage

Salon reached the zenith of its reputation in the late 1920s and 1930s, when it was the house wine at Maxim's. Nowadays, this champagne has a much more discreet image, but it is revered by certain connoisseurs, particularly in France, the United States and Great Britain, because the perfectionist wine-making principles of the founder are still followed to the letter, especially by the new owners of the firm, Laurent-Perrier, who took over in 1989.

The firm owns 2½ acres of vines at Le Mesnil which accounts for about one-fifth of its needs; the majority of the grapes are bought in from growers owning *grand cru* Mesnil plots in the village. Champagne-making is very traditional, the wines do not go through malolactic fermentation and are aged in wooden *demi-muid* casks. *Dégorgement à la volée* is still employed to preserve the aromas of the wines. The Salon house style is for rich, intensely fruity flavors with (say some) a whiff of walnuts, and strong life-giving acidity (a characteristic of all Mesnil champagnes). All Salon vintages need to be aged for at least 10 years before easing the cork.

⊕ Le Mesnil-sur-Oger

50,000 bottles

★★ the best quality available

A pannier presentation of Salon champagnes

My own experience of the wines is limited to one visit to the house in January 1994. But I was lucky enough to taste the 1983 and 1982 vintages, both with and without *dosage*. I have to say that owing to the superb natural ripeness of the grapes in each of the two vintages, the sugarless versions were splendid, and *extra brut* cuvées may well be released in future years. I loved the 1983 with its firm fresh attack and bell-like clarity of fruit; the 1982 was altogether richer and will probably have more fans, though I found it almost overripe and gamy (in the released version with *dosage*). Since 1911, vintages at Salon have been declared about three or four times a decade. Among these, the "greats" were, say the pundits, the toasty, perfectly balanced 1979; the fine-drawn 1973; the intense 1971 Cuvée "S"; the aromatic delicate 1969; the similarly subtle 1955; and the outstanding 1949. Of pre-war vintages, the 1928, of which there are some bottles in the cellar, is legendary.

Bertrand de Fleurian, Director of Salon

STYLES
PRESTIGE
CUVÉE "S" (1982)

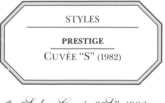

◀ *Salon Cuvée "S" 1982*

JACQUES SELOSSE

*Anselme Selosse, who heads this small 15-acre family
estate at Avize and Cramant, is one of the most interesting
growers in Champagne.*

A serious-minded fellow, turning 40, Anselme Selosse
trained at the Lycée Viticole in Beaune, and his orig-
inality has been to apply the hand-made approach of classic
white burgundy-making to the larger-scale, dare one say industrial, world of champagne. So at Jacques Selosse, the grapes
are hand-picked and the first fermentation always takes place
in oak vats or *barriques*; the wines remain on their lees for four
to six months and are stirred once a week with a baton *à la
Meursault* to give added character to the final flavors; and the
champagnes are given up to eight years' bottle age before
being disgorged – by hand, of course. One of Anselme's innovations has been his introduction of a *solera* system for the
reserve wine. In this system one-third of the reserve wine is
drawn off for use in the non-vintage cuvée, and replaced by
wine from the current vintage, so producing a reserve wine of
increasing complexity. The results are wines of inimitable
vinosity and original flavors that extend the taste spectrum of
champagne.

All Selosse champagnes are made from 100 percent Chardonnay grapes, are emphatically dry, and reflect the minerally,
chalky soil of Avize in their flavor. What puts them into the top
league is their Meursault-like *gras* tastes, which are always

Cuvée d'Origine 1987

Blanc de Blancs

beautifully balanced and never militate against finesse. A good introduction to the house style is the *Tradition Blanc de Blancs*, which has finesse and richness in equal measure and just the right amount of *dosage* to ease its definite dryness. The *Extra Brut Blanc de Blancs* is for aficionados of bone, bone dry, sugar-less champagne. It is a truly impressive wine of terrific complexity, but its awesome austerity will not appeal to everyone and it would benefit from keeping until 1995. Selosse also produces a wood-fermented *Rosé*, at once deep-flavored and elegant, and minuscule quantities of single-vintage champagnes from 1982, 1983, and 1985. However, all these delights pale by comparison with the *Cuvée d'Origine* 1987. First released in January 1994, this is Anselme's first cuvée made from wines fermented entirely in new, small, oak *barriques* – a fabulous, smoky, less austere wine with succulent orchard fruit flavors, it is a truly original tasting experience. Try it at L'Arpège Restaurant in Paris.

⊕	Avize
🍾	40,000 bottles
★★	the best quality available

STYLES
NON-VINTAGE
TRADITION BRUT BLANC DE BLANCS
EXTRA BRUT BLANC DE BLANCS
ROSÉ
ROSÉ
PRESTIGE
CUVÉE D'ORIGINE (1987)

◄ *Grand Cru Blanc de Blancs Brut*

T A I T T I N G E R

Taittinger's name as one of the most famous grandes
marques *is a relatively recent phenomenon, although
the firm can trace its origins back to 1743, when Jacques
Fourneaux went into the champagne business.*

During the First World War, Pierre Taittinger was billeted
as a French officer at the historic Château de la
Marqueterie near Epernay, which had been a favorite haunt
of Voltaire and Beaumarchais. After the Armistice, Pierre
bought the Château and its vineyards, and in the 1930s acquired
the defunct firm of Fourneaux, which he eventually renamed
Taittinger.

Since 1945, the firm has become one of the most important
new forces in the champagne world, thanks to the dynamism
of Pierre's two sons, François, who died in an accident in 1960,
and Claude, the current chairman of the company. The firm's
post-war expansion has been dramatic. It acquired the champagne house of Irroy in 1955; the Loire sparkling producer
Bouvet-Ladubay in 1973; the Concorde hotel chain in 1975;
and, most recently, Domaine Carneros in Napa Valley. The
firm also has interests in the construction and printing
industries.

Throughout its expansion, Taittinger has been an important
purchaser of vineyards, its current holdings now totalling 642

Presentation of Taittinger's Comtes de Champagne

Prestige Cuvée Comtes de Champagne Rosé 1986

Cuvée Prestige Rosé

Vintage Brut 1988

⬧ Reims

🍾 3.8 million bottles

★★ excellent quality

🍽 salmon with sorrel sauce

◀ *Taittinger Comtes de Champagne 1986*

```
┌─────────────────────────────────────────┐
│                 STYLES                    │
│                                           │
│   NON-VINTAGE          PRESTIGE           │
│   BRUT RÉSERVE        COMTES DE           │
│   ─────────           CHAMPAGNE BLANC     │
│   ROSÉ                DE BLANCS (1986)    │
│   BRUT PRESTIGE ROSÉ   TAITTINGER         │
│   VINTAGE              COLLECTION (1986,   │
│   VINTAGE BRUT (1988)    1985, 1978)      │
│                        COMTES DE          │
│                        CHAMPAGNE ROSÉ     │
│                          (1986)           │
└─────────────────────────────────────────┘
```

acres in the best sites of the Montagne de Reims and the Côte des Blancs. These account for half its needs. Although Taittinger is wary about revealing the exact grape composition of its cuvées, the style of the champagnes is strongly shaped by Chardonnay, with unmistakable floral aromas.

The non-vintage *Brut Réserve* can be a maddeningly variable champagne in my experience: sometimes it has a diffuse soapy taste; on other occasions it can be delightful, with soaring floral aromas and a poised, elegantly defined flavor. When last tasted in January 1994 it seemed to have quite a high *dosage*, which may give it street appeal but is likely to be less appealing to serious champagne buffs. I have no such reservations about the *Brut Prestige Rosé*, a subtle salmon-colored wine of real finesse driven by Chardonnay. With this wine the noticeable *dosage* seems a boon rather than a flaw.

The 1988 *Vintage Brut* is another slightly off-dry wine with a nice touch of maturity and complexity. The top-of-the-range *Comtes de Champagne Blanc de Blancs* 1986 is one of the best Chardonnay champagnes on the market, an expansively scented, silken-textured wine which will develop a near-burgundian nutty flavor with age: a marvellous partner for sauced fish dishes like salmon with sorrel sauce.

Taittinger's Collection champagnes are not just beautifully packaged deluxe items – the wines in the bottle can be superb, notably the 1978, the first in this series and decorated by the Hungarian artist Victor Vasarely. In the mid-1990s this wine has glorious ripe flavors of old Pinot Noir. More recently, the 1985 has a lovely design by the American Roy Lichtenstein and the 1986 one by Hans Hartung.

ALAIN THIÉNOT

Alain Thiénot is a man who gets things done. In his own quiet way, he is one of the most interesting characters on the French wine scene.

A former champagne broker, Alain Thiénot now has his own shipping house in Reims and two fine Bordeaux properties, Château Rahoul in the Graves and Château Ricaud in the Haut-Loupiac, where he makes lovely, sweet wine. Thiénot champagnes are rather like the man himself, natural, vital, with considerable strength of character. The firm owns 35 acres of vineyards which, although only accounting for about one-fifth of its needs, are mainly in *grand cru* sites such as Le Mesnil-sur-Oger and Ay.

STYLES

NON-VINTAGE	VINTAGE
BRUT	VINTAGE BRUT (1986)
ROSÉ	**PRESTIGE**
VINTAGE ROSÉ (1986)	GRANDE CUVÉE (1985)

Le Mesnil-sur-Oger on the Côte des Blancs

The non-vintage *Brut*, made from all three champagne grapes, shows good clear fruit, is fresh and sprightly, but the bubbles are not too aggressive. The 1986 vintage is nicely evolved with a nutty flavor while the *Grande Cuvée* 1985 is a true three-star champagne. With 20 percent fermentation in wood, there is real structure and complexity here, but the wine is so supple. It drinks beautifully and is something of a tribute to the blender's art; interestingly for a *Grande Cuvée* there is 10 percent Pinot Meunier in the blend. I am less keen on the Thiénot rosés, but the red still wine from Ay is recommended.

Brut N.V.

Grande Cuvée

⊕	Reims
🍾	550,000 bottles
★★	excellent quality

Grande Cuvée 1985: a beautifully balanced prestige Cuvée from a great year ▶

UNION CHAMPAGNE

Based in Avize on the Côte des Blancs, the Union de Champagne is the outstanding cooperative-conglomerate of the Champagne region, with a reputation for wines of excellent quality.

The Union Champagne is one of the region's relatively few cooperatives that exports its wines. The Union takes in grapes from 11 sub-cooperatives whose member-growers own prime vineyards mainly on the Côte des Blancs but with smaller holdings on the Montagne de Reims. Remarkably, all the growers' vineyards are classified as *premier cru* or *grand cru*, and only Pinot Noir and Chardonnay grapes are grown, with no plantings of the prolific but less fine Pinot Meunier.

The Union's vinification plant at Avize is probably the most modern in Champagne, and it has developed a special wine-making technique which avoids the malolactic fermentation, ensuring longer life and vitality in its champagnes.

The Union works well on several levels within the industry. About 60 percent of its annual production is the supply of still

Pierre Vaudon: a Pinot Noir-based Brut (Union Champagne)

wines (*vins clairs*) to the *grandes marques*. These wines contribute to the blends of such prestige cuvées as Taittinger *Comtes de Champagne*, Laurent-Perrier *Grand Siècle*, and Moët & Chandon *Dom Pérignon*.

The Union also markets about 40 percent of its production as finished champagnes for export, the best-known label being *St Gall*, which is imported by Marks & Spencer into Great Britain. Composed of 55 percent Pinot Noir and 45 percent Chardonnay, this cuvée has a fresh green-yellow color, a lively small-bubble *mousse* and a sprightly, definitely dry flavor.

The Union's best non-vintage cuvée is probably *Pierre Vaudon* because of the high proportion of Pinot Noir (70 percent) in the blend; it is soft, rich, round, and fine, and terrific value for money, selling for about $21 a bottle. The 1983 vintage *Orpale Blanc de Blancs* (100 percent Chardonnay) is a splendid wine with an almost white-Burgundy opulence; it recently came out on top in a blind tasting of prestige champagnes in Paris.

STYLES
NON-VINTAGE
PIERRE VAUDON
ST GALL
PRESTIGE
ORPALE BLANC DE BLANCS (1983)

✥ Avize

🍾 2 million bottles

★★ excellent quality

Pierre Vaudon (Union Champagne) ▶

VILMART

Tom Stevenson has called Vilmart the greatest
champagne grower he knows. Having visited this
perfectionist producer, I think he is right.

The house was founded in 1890 and is now run by René Champs and his son Laurent. They own 27 acres of *premier cru* Pinot Noir and Chardonnay, which they cultivate with an infinite capacity for taking pains. They use no chemical pesticides, even getting rid of the grass between the vines with a hand hoe. "Respecting our natural environment develops exceptional flavor in our wine," say the Champs. In the cellar, all the wines are fermented in oak casks, the vast majority of which are large *foudres*. Much of the range is aged for a very long time in bottle before *dégorgement*. The result is a brilliant repertoire of memorable champagnes of Krug-like richness, always balanced by exemplary acidity. To give you a measure of René Champs' character, his hobby is making stained-glass windows. Apparently it takes him 200 hours to create a single pane.

The Grande Réserve is a relatively young wine by Vilmart's standards. Made from 70 percent Pinot Noir and 30 percent

Cellar Museum of Wine at Vilmart

Chardonnay, about one-fifth of the must used comes from *première taille* pressings, as "this makes the wine round and gives it body;" it is then aged for 10 months in *foudres* before being given at least two years in bottle before release – a delightfully fruity, full-blown champagne which kills the myth that *all* good ones are made from the cuvée (very first pressings). The *Grand Cellier*, however, has more age, finesse, and class. With its lovely nutty bouquet and creamy richness, it will develop more complexities if kept in a cool cellar until 1995. The top-of-the-range *Grand Cellier d'Or*, though expensive, is worth every last penny, for its quality is on a par with prestige cuvées

Laurent and René Champs of Vilmart

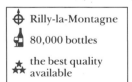

⊕ Rilly-la-Montagne

🍾 80,000 bottles

★★ the best quality available

Coeur de Cuvée 1989: a top cuvée made from the best first pressings of the grapes ▶

from the greatest houses. It is splendidly rounded on the nose with a whiff of *pain d'épices*, and its honeyed opulence in the mouth is wonderful.

The latest releases from Vilmart are its innovative *Coeur de Cuvée* champagnes; as the name implies, the wine comes from the best part, "the heart" of the cuvée. The 1989 has extraordinary complexity and vinosity; the *barrique*-fermented 1991, last tasted in January 1994, has a strong overlay of woody flavours and I would like to taste it again before judging its future potential. The house also produces good rosé champagnes, the *Grand Cellier* having more class than the *Cuvée Rubis*.

Vilmart is typical of smaller grower-producers (*récoltant-manipulant*) in that their main business remains within the domestic French market. In the economic recession of the 1990s they suffered less of a fall in sales than many of their colleagues in the business.

Stained-glass cellar window at Vilmart

STYLES

NON-VINTAGE
GRANDE RÉSERVE
GRAND CELLIER
ROSÉ
RUBIS BRUT
GRAND CELLIER RUBIS

PRESTIGE
GRAND CELLIER D'OR
COEUR DE CUVÉE
(1989, 1991)

Vilmart Grand Cellier

Grand Cellier D'Or

Grande Réserve

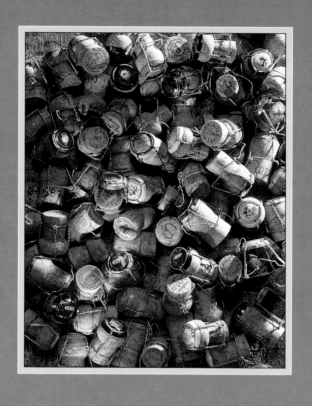

= 3 =

DIRECTORY OF
LESSER KNOWN
Champagne
PRODUCERS

BESSERAT DE BELLEFON

Until 1959, Besserat de Bellefon was a family business best known for its *crémant* (gently sparkling) champagnes. Since then the firm has had several corporate owners (Marne et Champagne is the most recent), and sales have been rapidly expanded to over 2 million bottles a year. The Besserat house style is for light, fresh wines with no trace of oxidation, though you have to pick and choose to find the best bottles. The standard *Brut* is lean and ungenerous and should be avoided. The Chardonnay-dominated *Crémant Blanc Brut*, with its gentle sparkle and creamy flavor, makes a good aperitif, while the *Cuvée des Moines Rosé* has great finesse, thanks to a significant proportion of Chardonnay in the blend. Easily the finest champagne in the range is the prestige *Grande Cuvée B de B*, a blend of several years, which has plenty of body but remains fresh and clean in the house style.

 Epernay
2.2 million bottles
★ good quality

BINET

An important house in its own right during the 19th century, Binet is now the upmarket brand for Champagne Germain, based in Rilly-la-Montagne, and is sold to specialist outlets rather than supermarkets. Good Pinot-Noir dominated *Rosé*.

Rilly-la-Montagne
500,000 bottles
★ good quality

BONAPARTE

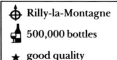

Secondary *marque* of Napoléon, a brand sold in Russia at the turn of the century by the Prieur family who still run the business. Quality wine-making and adherence to traditional methods. The *Special Réserve Brut* is recommended.

 Vertus
160,000 bottles
★ good quality

BONNET

Although now owned by
Charles Heidsieck (a member
of the Rémy-Cointreau group),
the house of Ferdinand
Bonnet, established in the
1920s, was run by the family
until 1988. It has 25 acres of
excellent vineyards on the Côte
des Blancs at Avize, Oger, and
Vertus. The house produces
Chardonnay-dominated wines
with stylish vintage-selection
Blanc de Blancs.

Oger

150,000 bottles

★ good quality

BOUCHE

This is a small independent
house near Epernay, with 74
acres of vineyards spread across
ten *échelle des crus*. The house
produces good, generously
flavored champagne, naturally
brut non-vintage, and excellent,
vanilla-rich *Cuvée Saphir* which
is made from *grand cru* grapes
(60 percent Pinot Noir, 40
percent Chardonnay).

Pierry

250,000 bottles

★ good quality

BOUCHERON

The second label of Gardet,
Boucheron are traditionally
minded producers specializing
in champagnes with long bottle
age. They produce a big,
vinous, Pinot-Noir driven style
champagne, sourced from

high-class grapes from
vineyards mainly on the
Montagne de Reims. The
Boucheron *Brut* non-vintage
won a gold medal at the 1993
International Wine Challenge.
The house produces superb
1983 vintage wine.

Chigny-les-Roses

600,000 bottles

★★ excellent quality

CATTIER

Vignerons since the mid-18th century, the Cattiers founded this small champagne firm in 1920. A 44-acre *domaine* around Chigny-Les-Roses supplies most of the grapes for these thoroughly decent champagnes, which are properly aged in the bottle before release. The *Premier Cru*, composed of three-quarters black grapes and a quarter Chardonnay, is elegant, sprightly, but with a nice touch of maturity and vinous

complexity. The 5.4-acre walled vineyard, the *Clos du Moulin* provides the best wine: a 50/50 mix of Pinot Noir and Chardonnay, it has an inviting smell of fresh-baked bread and an excellent fruit-to-acid balance on the palate with a long persistent finish.

⊕	Chigny-les-Roses
🍾	400,000 bottles
★	good quality

COCTEAUX

From a family of Sézannais growers, Michel Cocteaux started his own vineyard at Montgenost in 1964 and now farms 22 acres of predominantly Chardonnay grapes. Cocteaux's champagnes are very delicate and long-flavored. Successful *Cuvée Trentenaire* 1987.

⊕	Montgenost
🍾	55,000 bottles
★	good quality

DE LA HAYE

These champagnes are made for the label de la Haye by an anonymous grower-producer in Epernay. The wines have fanciful names like "Wedding Cuvée." Generally only fair quality, though the *Robert de la Haye Brut* non-vintage is a very good champagne made from *premier cru* grapes.

⊕	Epernay
🍾	300,000 bottles
★	acceptable quality

DE MERIC

A smallish merchant/grower founded in 1960 by Christian Besserat, with 37 acres of vines at Ay. *Sélection Brut* (mainly Pinot Noir) is a fine, non-vintage champagne, natural, dry, with good fruit definition.

- ⊕ Ay
- 🍾 450,000 bottles
- ★ good quality

PAUL DE RICHEBOURGE

No, this artfully named wine is not a burgundy but a second champagne label of the excellent Union Auboise in Bar-sur-Seine. The *Brut* non-vintage is a great value and has three to four years' bottle age.

- ⊕ Bar-sur-Seine
- 🍾 1.8 million bottles
- ★ good quality

LOUIS DE SACY

Vignerons in Champagne since the 17th century, the de Sacy's became *négociants* in the 1960s. With 74 acres of vineyards planted with mainly Pinot Noir, the house style is black-grape dominated.

- ⊕ Verzy
- 🍾 300,000 bottles
- ★ good quality

DELOT

Small grower in the Aube with mainly Pinot Noir grapes. Strict adherence to traditional methods produces full, rich champagnes that are good value for money. The *Grande Réserve Brut* is well rounded and delicious.

- ⊕ Celles-sur-Ources
- 🍾 40,000 bottles
- ★ good quality

DUVAL LEROY

Founded in 1859, this dynamic *négociant* house is a big player in the "Buyer's Own Brand" business, particularly in Great Britain, where its champagnes appear under supermarket labels. Duval Leroy's own *Fleur de Champagne Brut*, made with 75 percent Chardonnay, is a stylish, flower-scented wine which regularly upstages the competition from the *grandes marques*.

⊕ Vertus

🍾 4 million bottles

★ good quality

ROLAND FLINIAUX

A highly traditional, little, family-run firm, now run by Régis Fliniaux. The house's small 7-acre vineyard of *grand cru* Pinot Noir at Ay produces wines in a full-blooded, uncompromising style that is the Fliniaux signature throughout the range. The champagnes are still disgorged by hand. The *Carte Noire Brut* is gutsy and the wild strawberry-scented *Rosé* is superb.

⊕ Ay

🍾 74,000 bottles

★★ excellent quality

Aube vineyards

GAUTHIER

Gauthier is one of the better labels from the anonymous champagne-producing giant, Marne et Champagne. The *Grande Réserve Brut* should be sought out. It is made from all three champagne grapes with a slight predominance of Chardonnay, the latter shaping the racy, lemony flavors of a well-balanced yet lively wine.

⊕ Epernay

🍾 200,000 bottles

★ good quality

RENÉ GEOFFROY

Grower/producer with *premier cru* holdings in the Vallée de la Marne using traditional methods, such as part fermentation in wood and late disgorging of vintage champagnes. The *Cuvée Sélectionnée Brut* (6–7 years' bottle age) is good and the *Cumières Rouge* excellent.

⊕ Cumières

🍾 110,000 bottles

★★ excellent quality

HENRI GERMAIN

Established in 1895 by Henri-Antoine Germaine, the firm is now owned by the Frey group; the champagnes are sold under the Germain and Binet labels. Germain owns 99 acres of vineyards, accounting for 40 percent of its needs. Recommended: the sprightly long-flavored 1988 *Blanc de Blancs* and the fruit-laden *Rosé Brut*.

 Rilly-la-Montagne

 1.2 million bottles

★ good quality

PIERRE GIMONNET

Growers in Cuis since the 18th century, the Gimmonets now own 62 acres of choice Chardonnay sites on the Côte des Blancs. Finesse marks this range of *Blanc de Blancs*. The exciting, vital *Maxi-Brut* (without *dosage*) and the newly released *Cuvée Gastronome* 1989 are particular wines to earmark. Gimmonet wines are excellent for matching with food.

⊕ Cuis

🍾 140,000 bottles

★★ excellent quality

HENRI GOUTORBE

With 49 acres of vineyards at Ay, the Goutorbes are both vine nurserymen and producers of their own champagnes in a Pinot-dominated style. The *Cuvée Traditionelle* is a reliable, well-balanced wine "lifted" by a little Chardonnay. The *Rosé* is full of black-grape fruitiness, and the *Spécial Club 1986* is powerful with excellent acidity. Small quantities of old vintages under *Millésime Rare* label.

⊕ Ay

🍾 120,000 bottles

★★ excellent quality

GREMILLET

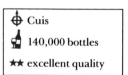

J-M Gremillet is typical of the better class Aube producer, making excellent champagnes from low-yielding Pinot Noir and Chardonnay vines. From 30 acres of choice Chardonnay sites he makes a very fine *Brut Réserve* with four years' bottle age, a great Pinot Noir *Rosé*, and a first-class *Blanc de Blancs*.

⊕ Balnot-sur-Laignes

🍾 100,000 bottles

★★ excellent quality

JEANMAIRE

Sharing the same modern premises as Oudinot, and owned by the Trouillard family, Jeanmaire makes technically correct champagnes in a light, flowery style. The *Brut* non-vintage is a clean-tasting wine of decent bottle age. The firm owns altogether 197 acres of vineyards.

⊕ Epernay

🍾 1 million bottles

★ good quality

LANG BIÉMONT

Founded in 1875, Lang Biémont produces half a million bottles of champagne a year in a light, Chardonnay-influenced style. The firm owns 123 acres of vineyards on the Côte des Blancs. The 100 percent Chardonnay *Cuvée d'Exception* is recommended.

⊕ Oiry

🍾 500,000 bottles

★ good quality

Chalk carvings of a vigneron

LAURENT

A small Aube grower making very good value Pinot Noir-dominated *Brut* non-vintage, and interesting older wines like a *1981 Blanc de Noirs*.

⊕ Celles-sur-Ources

🍾 55,000 bottles

★ good quality

LAURENTI

Papa Laurenti and sons Dominique and Bruno run this 35-acre vineyard at Les Riceys, planted with 90 percent Pinot Noir and 10 percent Chardonnay. The *Brut Grande Cuvée* and its pink brother are full of red fruit flavors.

🜨 Les Riceys

🍾 100,000 bottles

★ good quality

ALBERT LE BRUN

Originally established at Avize in 1860, Albert le Brun is a fine family business. Their traditional, big, rich wines offer very good value for the money. The *Blanc de Blancs Brut* is a ripe, smoky wine from the firm's vineyards at Avize.

🜨 Châlons-sur-Marne

🍾 350,000 bottles

★ good quality

LE BRUN DE NEUVILLE

A small cooperative on the Coteaux des Sézannais, now building its own bottle sales. Nearly all the grapes are Chardonnay. They produce full, fruity wines. The *Blanc de Blancs* non-vintage is a good value.

🜨 Bethon

🍾 500,000 bottles

★ good quality

LECLERC-BRIANT

This family firm with fine vineyards is run by Pascal Leclerc-Briant. *Les Authentiques Collection* are champagnes made from small parcels of vines in specific sites, in a vinous, near-Burgundian style.

🜨 Epernay

🍾 300,000 bottles

★ good quality

LENOBLE

Founded in 1920, A. R. Lenoble owns 44 acres of mainly Chardonnay vineyards. The *Cuvée Réserve*, unusually 60 percent Chardonnay and 40 percent Pinot Meunier, is a big, golden champagne, rounded and just off-dry.

⊕ Damery

🍾 300,000 bottles

★ good quality

Village in the Champagne wine field

SERGE MATHIEU

Serge Mathieu makes velvety, hedonistic champagnes, which sweep the board at blind tastings. The *Cuvée Sélect*, made entirely from 1989 vintage grapes, has a superb balance of richness and elegance.

⊕ Avirey-Lingey

🍾 90,000 bottles

★★ excellent quality

MELNOTTE

Sous-marque of Boizel, this is a champagne produced for the London shipper O. W. Loeb. Good-value, straightforward *Brut*, excellent *Rosé*, and a sprightly, well-made *1986 Brut*.

⊕ Epernay

🍾 50,000 bottles

★ good quality

JULES MIGNON

Jules Mignon is one of several hundred brands produced by Marne et Champagne, the second biggest stockholder of wines in Champagne. No money is spent on promoting the firm, so merchants and especially supermarkets buy from this source when they want to buy a champagne of a certain style at a price they can afford under a label of their choice. Marne et Champagne dominates this "Buyer's Own Brand" sector of the champagne business. Quality varies widely from green, unripe champagnes to genuinely fine offerings. When I asked the British agent to send a sample of *Rothschild*, a champagne I have always liked since being a trainee at Marne et Champagne in 1968, he dispatched two wines under the *Alfred Rothschild* prestige label. Both the *Jules Mignon Brut* and the *Jules Mignon Rosé* tasted green and immature and are not recommended.

 Epernay

10 million bottles

★ average quality

PIERRE MONCUIT

Lucky Yves and Nicole Moncuit own 49 acres in Le Mesnil-sur-Oger, the "Corton-Charlemagne" of the Côte des Blancs. Their talent is as big as their birthright. They make a range of extremely incisive *Blanc de Blancs* of great class.

Le Mesnil-sur-Oger

120,000 bottles

★★ excellent quality

MONTAUDON

This firm, established in 1891, is run by Luc Montaudon, the great-grandson of the founder. Good long-lived *Grande Réserve Rosé* and the red *Coteaux Champenois Rouge* sourced from the firm's 50 acres of Pinot Noir grapes.

 Reims

700,000 bottles

★ good quality

MONTEBELLO

This firm was founded in 1834 at the imposing Château de Mareuil-sur-Ay by the Duc de Montebello, the son of Napoleon's general, Maréchal Lannes. It is owned by Ayala and is quite overshadowed by its parent. Champagnes not tasted. Since 1994, no longer a *grande marque*.

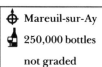

- ⊕ Mareuil-sur-Ay
- 🍾 250,000 bottles
- not graded

MICHEL NOIROT

Michel Noirot makes excellent, pure-flavored champagnes – as near as possible to being organic – primarily from black grapes. The *Cuvée du Clos St. Roche* is a first-rate bottle, elegant, stylish, and persistent on the palate, with five to six years' bottle age and a majority of Chardonnay in the blend.

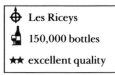

- ⊕ Les Riceys
- 🍾 150,000 bottles
- ★★ excellent quality

OUDINOT

Since 1981, Oudinot has been owned by the Trouillard family and shares an ultra-modern winery with Jeanmaire, producing an across-the-board range to suit all tastes. Oudinot is an important owner of vineyards in key villages, with five holdings in Avize, Cramant, and Chouilly.

Generally attractive Pinot Noir-dominated wines with a fine *Blanc de Noirs*. A popular brand in the United States.

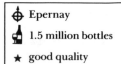

- ⊕ Epernay
- 🍾 1.5 million bottles
- ★ good quality

MARIE STUART

Housed in an impressive building on Reims' Place de la République, Marie Stuart makes light, straightforward champagnes, many of which appear under "Buyer's Own Brand" labels. Decent 1986 vintage champagne.

⊕	Reims
🍾	1.7 million bottles
★	acceptable quality

MARCEL VÉZIEN

Vézien, mayor of Celles-sur-Ource (Aube) makes full, lush champagne redolent of orchard fruit. Pinot Noir accounts for as much as 80 percent of the cuvées. The sensational *Cuvée Double Eagle II*, a sensuous Pinot mouthful, was named after American balloonists who celebrated their safe arrival on French soil with a bottle of this nectar.

⊕	Celles-sur-Ource
🍾	150,000 bottles
★★	excellent quality

VRANKEN-LAFITTE

Established in 1976 by Paul-François Vranken, a resourceful Belgian entrepreneur, this is now a large champagne house with a multiplicity of labels. The most widely distributed brand is "Desmoiselle," though the best wines appear under the "Charles Lafitte" label (very good *Rosé* 1986). The company has recently acquired the Barancourt Champagne house of Bouzy.

⊕	Epernay
🍾	3 million bottles
★	good quality

Glossary

assemblage The blending of wines.
autolysis Biochemical process in which yeast cells are broken down. In champagne production it occurs during the *prise de mousse*, adding a vital complexity to the finished taste.
barrique A small oak barrel of about 50 gallons capacity.
cave A cellar – usually underground in Champagne.
chef de caves Cellarmaster: person responsible for the production of champagne in the cellars. Usually a qualified oenologist (wine scientist) in charge of blending.
CM A champagne that has been made by a cooperative. See also **cooperative-manipulante.**
coopérative-manipulante (CM) A cooperative making and marketing champagne.
Coteaux Champenois Appellation (controlled name of origin) for still white, rosé, and red wines produced in the Champagne winefield. Known as "Vin nature de Champagne" before 1973.
crayère Gallo-Roman chalk pit used as a champagne cellar in Reims.
Crémant In Champagne, traditionally a gently sparkling wine under approximately 3.5 atmospheres of pressure. From August 1994 the champagne houses are forbidden to use the word on the main label.
cru Wine, usually high quality, from a specific commune or village.
cuvée 1 The first 455 gallons of pressed grape juice. 2 A champagne blend.
débourbage Separation of pressed grape juice from solid matter prior to fermentation.
dégorgement The elimination of the deposit in a bottle of champagne following its second fermentation.
dégorgement à la glace The bottle

passes neck-down through freezing brine and the deposit is expelled as a pellet of ice when the cork or crown cap is removed. **dégorgement à la volée** Disgorging by hand without freezing.
demi-muid An oak cask of 132 gallons capacity.
dosage Sugared liqueur added to a bottle of champagne to soften the wine. Expressed in percentages or in grams of sugar per liter.
échelle de cru Classification of the Champagne crus or communes expressed on a percentage scale. It is geographically based but is essentially an index of price, based on the quality of grapes from individual vineyards. The poorest rate 77 percent; deuxième crus rate 80–89 percent; premiers crus 90–99 percent; grands crus 100 percent.
foudre Large wooden cask of no standard size.
grand cru One of 17 Champagne villages rated 100 percent on the échelle de cru.
grande marque A leading champagne house belonging to the Syndicat des Grandes Marques ("great brands") founded in 1882. Currently made up of some 25 member houses.
gyropalette An automatic remuage (riddling) system: a "palette" or metal container holding up to 500 bottles.
lees Sediment – the by-products of fermentation – that falls to the floor of the vat in the wine-making process.
liqueur de tirage A liqueur based on sugar and yeasts, added to still wine at bottling to make it sparkle.
malolactic fermentation Conversion of tart malic acid into milder lactic acid to make wines softer and rounder.
méthode champenoise "Champagne method." The traditional way of

making champagne and other quality sparkling wines. Still wine is made sparkling by a second fermentation in the bottle. Under new EC rules the term is being replaced by "*méthode traditionalle*."

méthode rurale The earliest known method of making sparkling wine, attributed to Benedictine monks in Limoux in the 16th century. Incompletely fermented wine is put into a bottle to make it sparkle.

millésime The year of the vintage.

millésimé In Champagne, the wine of a single year sold after at least three years in the bottle.

monocru Unblended champagne from a single cru (commune or village). Most champagnes from small growers (récoltants-manipulant) fall into this category.

mousse Bubbles.

mousseux A fully sparkling wine under 5 to 6 atmospheres of pressure.

négociant-manipulant (NM) A merchant (*négociant*) who is permitted to buy grapes or wines for blends from other sources. Some or all of the wines in a blend may come from the négociant-manipulant's own vineyard. All the famous champagne houses are NMs.

NM Champagne from a négociant-manipulant.

NV Non-vintage.

premier cru In Champagne a wine-growing commune with a 90–99 per-cent rating on the échelle des crus.

prise de mousse Second fermentation in the bottle due to the addition of sugar and yeast liqueur to the still wine at bottling.

pupitre wooden racks for remuage.

RC Champagne produced by a récoltant-coopérateur.

RD *récemment dégorgé* ("recently disgorged.") Applied to very high quality champagnes, usually from single vintages, which have been aged in the bottle for a long time. They are disgorged a few months before release. The term "RD" has been patented by Bollinger, the leading producer of this type of champagne.

récoltant-coopérateur (RC) A small grower without the means to vinify champagne, who has it made from his or her own grapes by one or more cooperatives and sells the finished champagne under his or her own label. Champagne labelled RC is not truly a grower's wine as grapes from the récoltant-coopérateur may be blended with others.

récoltant-manipulant (RM) A small grower making champagne from his or her grapes but allowed to buy in 5 percent from other sources.

remuage Riddling. The careful turning and tilting of bottles of champagne so the deposit formed as a by-product of the second fermentation may settle on the cork. It is expelled from the bottle by dégorgement. See also **gyropalette; pupitre.**

reserve wines Older wines than those from the current vintage kept in reserve to contribute harmonious balance to a champagne blend.

RM Champagne produced by a récoltant-manipulant.

SR Société de Récoltant: a company formed by wine growers belonging to the same family who want to pool resources.

sur lattes 1 Champagnes that have been stored on their sides. 2 Near-finished champagnes awaiting dégorgement, which are sold on by the producer and labeled as the buyer's own product.

taille: première taille The second pressings of champagne grapes (90 gallons). **deuxième taille** The third pressings of champagne grapes (45 gallons). Now effectively abolished in Champagne.

tête de cuvée The finest juice from the first pressings of grapes.

vendange Harvest.

vigneron A wine grower.

Index